National and Regional Parliaments in the European Constitutional Order

Edited by Philipp Kiiver

Europa Law Publishing is a publishing company
specializing in European Union Law.
For further information please contact Europa Law
Publishing via email: info@europalawpublishing.com
or visit our website at: www.europalawpublishing.com.

Typeset in Scala and Scala Sans, Graphic design by
G2K Designers, Groningen/Amsterdam

NUR 828
ISBN-10: 90-76871-63-9
ISBN-13: 978-90-76871-63-9

British Library Cataloguing-in-Publication Data
A catalogue record for this book is available from the
British Library

National and Regional Parliaments in the European Constitutional Order

Europa Law Publishing, Groningen 2006

Acknowledgements

All but one of the chapters in this volume are based on contributions to a workshop that was held on 2 December 2005 at Edinburgh during the annual conference of the Ius Commune research school. For both the organisation of the workshop and the preparation of this volume I could always count on the support of Ius Commune, as well as the *Breedtestrategie* fund for public law research. I am thankful to Prof. Michael Faure and Prof. Luc Verhey of Maastricht University for ensuring this support. I am furthermore thankful to the authors, as well as to Jacqueline Lensink at Europa Law Publishing, for their diligence, commitment and enthusiasm. The result is not only an enlightening, but also a very much timely piece of work.

Philipp Kiiver
Maastricht, April 2006

The editor
Dr. Philipp Kiiver
Assistant Professor of European and Comparative Constitutional Law, Maastricht University

The authors
Prof. Leonard Besselink
Jean Monnet Chair of European Constitutional Law, University of Utrecht

Dr. Caitríona Carter
Senior Lecturer, Europa Institute, University of Edinburgh

Dr. Adam Cygan
Senior Lecturer, Faculty of Law, Centre for European Law and Integration, University of Leicester

Dr. Gordon Heggie
Lecturer, University of Strathclyde, Glasgow

Mr. Wouter Pas
Auditor, Belgian Council of State / Scientific collaborator, Institute for Constitutional Law, Catholic University of Leuven

Prof. Siniša Rodin
Professor of European Public Law, University of Zagreb

Dr. Olaf Tans
Postdoc-Researcher, Department of Constitutional and Administrative Law, University of Amsterdam

CHAPTER I

Parliaments, Regions and European Integration

Fresh Perspectives on the European Constitutional Order

Philipp Kiiver

1 Introduction

The title of this volume begs for an explanation: just what do we mean by 'national and regional parliaments', what is a 'European constitutional order', and what do the former have to do with the latter? What is the link between regions, member states, parliaments, governments, and the European Union? The question is a complex one, and accordingly the answers that can be given are manifold. First, the answers would of course depend on the discipline one works in as a main scholarly framework, such as political science, European or constitutional law. Second, they would strongly depend on the national perspective one takes: practical or conceptual problems arising from the involvement of parliaments in European affairs can be perceived as irrelevant or simply not applicable in one country, but as real and pressing in another.

Take as an example the parliament of the United Kingdom: the political priority there remains how Westminster can better steer and hold to account British ministers for their European policies. Parliament's communication with devolved regions in the UK is an issue, but not one of any primary concern. To the Scottish parliament, however, this is exactly what needs to be addressed if a Scottish dimension is to be inserted in British national representation in Brussels. To hyper-federalised Belgium, finding sometimes unorthodox solutions how to accommodate its powerful regions and communities is a continuous challenge; to the Netherlands, a unitary state with limited decentralisation, regions are meanwhile far less of an issue. What is usually more pressing is, again, the question how to arrange and enforce ministerial responsibility to parliament in EU matters. Usually, that is. For since the negative referendum result on the EU Constitutional Treaty in 2005, the integration-friendly Dutch political establishment in parliament now had better sort out how to provide for a better embedding of EU policies in Dutch society, rather than fixating on government-parliament relations only. Ministerial responsibility of course nevertheless remains a central and contentious point, not only in the Netherlands, be it that it is not always a *lack* of parliamentary oversight that is considered problematic: in Croatia, a country that prepares for EU accession, the government actually seems to be tied *too much* to parliamentary control in the field of external and European relations. Parliaments can thus also 'overdo it' when it comes to enforcing involvement in EU matters. Yet does parliamentary participation actually only hinge on whether ministerial accountability at the domestic level is weak or strong, too lenient or too restrictive? Not necessarily, one might argue, since there is little, in terms of formal obstacles, that would prevent national and also regional parliaments from engaging in direct cross-border dialogues, and in non-mediated dialogues with the EU institutions already. This is where we need to reconsider our understanding of constitutional hierarchies within the member states, and also the European Union at large.

To allow for a view that is both cross-discipline and cross-country in nature, the present volume brings together authors from both law and political science, and offers perspectives which illustrate how notions regarding parliamentarism and European integration vary from one region to another, one member state to another, between member states and candidate countries, and between different conceptual approaches to understanding and developing the EU itself. Giving a mere summary of all contributions to the present volume would mean to miss much of the complexity and subtlety of the individual chapters. It is however possible to offer some common threads. Here I shall elaborate *three themes* along which we might link, and contrast with each other, the individual contributions: first, the regional dimension of parliamentarism in Europe, and the link between sub-national parliaments and EU decision-making; second, the notion that parliamentary participation can, does, or should go beyond the confines of domestic ministerial accountability, and that parliaments, but also governments, might 'break free' from these constitutional constraints; third, a critical re-assessment of EU treaty-drafting exercises in the light of parliamentary participation, the Convention method, the different priorities parliaments set when influencing treaty-making, and the role that they play at the ratification stage. Again, not all themes are equally central to each national perspective; yet it is exactly the variety of national views and conceptual approaches that characterises Europe as a dynamic, polycentric, and very much multi-faceted polity.

2 The Regional Dimension of Parliamentarism

As noted, the fact that a member state has gone though a process of decentralisation or devolution does not necessarily imply that this becomes the most salient issue in the national parliament as regards giving a regional dimension to EU policy-formulation. In his contribution on the United Kingdom, Adam Cygan illustrates how Westminster, both the Commons and the Lords, mainly concentrate their efforts on obtaining relevant EU-related information for themselves, and on preventing ministers from agreeing prematurely to EU measures in the Council, that is before the Commons and Lords have duly completed scrutiny. Although the principle of subsidiarity, that is regulation at the lowest sensible level, does not stop at the national level but extends to regions, the receipt of input from the devolved entities in the UK does not seem to get priority treatment, at least not in Westminster. What is offered, as Gordon Heggie in his contribution on the Scottish parliament elaborates, are facilities to channel Scottish views to the UK government and the EU under a principle of 'partnership'. The meaningful realisation of such an approach is however impaired by two typical constraints. The first is the gap between the centre and the regions in a state that features devolution but is not fully federalised: Scottish ministers may accompany British ministers to the Council, yet essentially EU decision-making remains an issue of national, that is UK, external relations. The second constraint is the gap between parliament and government: in a field of national executive prerogatives, parliaments have to insist on involvement if they do not wish to be marginalised. This applies to the Scottish parliament's links to both the UK government and its own Scottish executive: the UK government may consult the Scottish executive, but the involvement of the Scottish *parliament* in these consultations is an entirely different question. The centre-region and government-parliament gap, when combined, lead to a situation where the involvement of the Scottish parliament in EU matters is mediated, and mitigated, by the Scottish executive, the Westminster parliament, and the UK government.

If EU involvement remains a pressing issue to the Scottish parliament, then it would either have to overcome the obstacles on the domestic scene, or circumnavigate these obstacles, or both. The circumnavigation would imply an entertainment of direct Scottish links to the EU institutions, to other governments, and to other regions in Europe, bypassing London. Some of these features are already present, some more developed than others. One example is the region-Commission dialogue over EU regional funds; another is the proto-network of regional parliaments in the European Union.

To the sub-national assemblies in Belgium, meanwhile, the perspective of a 'principle of partnership' with the federal government in EU matters would almost amount to an insult. As Wouter Pas in his contribution compellingly demonstrates, the high degree of federalisation within Belgium has had a strong impact on Belgian policy-formulation and representation in the EU; in fact it challenges the Union's understanding of what is or should be considered as a 'national parliament'. The starting point in Belgium is that the federal authority, as well as the sub-national entities, the regions and communities, are placed on an equal footing under Belgian constitutional law. The exercise of domestic competences is not governed by federal supremacy over sub-national law, but by a strict separation of competences, so that any one competence can be allocated only to one entity at a time, the entities being co-equal. And where an entity, federal or sub-national, is competent domestically, it is also competent externally, including the field of EU relations. For Belgian representation in the Council this implies that, subject to ingenious domestic co-ordination procedures, Belgium's seat can be taken up by sub-national ministers. Regarding the facilities offered by the Constitutional Treaty to national parliaments, especially the right to information and the binding and non-binding veto powers awarded to national parliaments, this means that solutions had, and still have to be found how to reconcile Belgian federalism with EU treaty-making. Since Belgium does not fit the bicameral blueprint, but insists that all its federal and sub-national assemblies together form one big multi-cameral national parliament, we are prompted to explore the boundaries of national sovereignty, constitutional autonomy, regionalism, and the EU's desire to give national parliaments a more prominent role.

National parliaments are thus not only central parliaments: there is a distinct regional dimension to EU exercises to promote parliamentarism in the member states. This is especially so as regards the principle of subsidiarity. Caitríona

Carter, in her spicy rejoinder to the contributions on the UK and Scotland, calls for greater attention to the question how subsidiarity can be operationalised in practice, and how workable criteria as to compliance or non-compliance can be developed. Whether subsidiarity is a veritable commitment in EU decision-making, or merely a soft-law bone that is thrown to parliaments in the member states, to a large extent depends on the principle's practical workability. The degree to which the guardianship of subsidiarity is spread out to sub-national actors, or is restricted to central parliaments, will also tell us something about the degree to which the principle is taken at all seriously.

3 Breaking Free from Ministerial Accountability

A second thread in the present discussion can be summarised as follows: to what extent is the involvement of parliaments in EU matters dependent on the notion of ministerial accountability? Or, to put it differently, is there any way that parliaments, governments, EU institutions, and scholarly observers, can explore avenues of participation outside this specific aspect of domestic government-parliament relations?

True, where a cabinet depends on the confidence or tolerance of a parliamentary majority to stay in office and conduct policies, the government can be made subject to parliamentary scrutiny, steering and control. At least theoretically, this also applies to the field of EU policies, which parliament might try to influence *ex ante*, by pressing Brussels-bound ministers, and on which parliament might want to hear justifications *ex post*, by calling ministers to account upon their return. In fact, this is still the primary avenue chosen by the parliament of the UK, already for thirty years of EC/EU membership. Following the path of the domestic legislative process, Westminster would insist on receiving EU drafts and proposals for scrutiny and consideration. To make sure that the minister does not pre-empt the parliament by quickly agreeing to EU measures in the Council, a scrutiny reserve is put into operation which restricts ministers' freedom to agree in Brussels pending domestic scrutiny. As Adam Cygan argues, Westminster thereby seeks to compensate a loss of sovereignty in domestic law-making with additional scrutiny of ministers: scrutiny becomes a form of 'substitute sovereignty'. The Scottish parliament, by contrast, is in a far weaker position as regards the UK government, if only for the fact that British ministers are not accountable to devolved assemblies. Formal obligations to provide information, let alone scrutiny reserves, are thus problematic to impose. Direct Scottish links to EU institutions then become the avenue of choice. This is an effort that is pragmatically made because the informal working of the 'principle of partnership' with the central authority in London is, as Gordon Heggie argues, at times frustrating, especially to Scottish parliamentarians. In addition, this effort of developing direct and unmitigated links also forms part, as Caitríona

Carter notes, of a more fundamental process whereby the still relatively young Scottish parliament tries to find its place within the UK and EU order.

Needless to say that sub-national assemblies in Belgium have no way of enforcing ministerial accountability of federal ministers either: accountability and confidence relates to their respective sub-national ministers only, not to the federal cabinet. In fact that is not even necessary since a situation is achieved whereby, say, the Flemish parliament, in areas of exclusive Flemish competences, is put on par with the federal Belgian parliament for EU purposes. Other member states are already used to working with sub-national ministers representing Belgium, and other federal member states, in the Council. Yet they might still have to get used to the idea that federalism applies not only to governments but also to parliaments, and that the sub-national assemblies form part of the Belgian 'national parliament'. Such acceptance may swiftly come to an end when it comes to subjecting EU decisions to national parliamentary vetoes, as envisaged by the EU Constitutional Treaty under, very importantly, the simplified treaty revision clause that can be vetoed by any one national parliament or chamber. It would be intriguing to see whether other member states would accept a Flemish 'no' against the application of the clause as a binding vote blocking a European Council decision.

Yet ministerial accountability is not only put into a relative perspective when it comes to regions. National parliaments themselves might yet come to realise that engaging in EU policies does not always have to mean to just put pressure on their own ministers. The real impact of parliaments, majorities and minorities therein, is anyway generally limited for various reasons which lie both in domestic arrangements and the logic of executive federalism in the EU. Apart from that, real parliamentary impact on governmental EU policy is difficult to measure empirically, as Caitríona Carter stresses in her contribution. A most intriguing train of thought is then that, at least formally, little stands in the way of an active participation of parliamentary actors in the EU, without the dominant governments standing in between. A key to opening up to new routes of participation would be, as Leonard Besselink argues in his thought-provoking contribution, to reconsider the implications of the notion of multi-level governance. The 'levels' paradigm, as in 'multilevel governance' or 'multilevel constitutionalism', has already successfully opened our view of the European Union as a polity that is governed by non-hierarchical interactions between and across layers of government. Yet we are now invited to take the next step, and free ourselves from the semantic grip of 'levels', which still imply that even though interaction takes place, European and national constitutional orders remain autonomous with respect to each other. Instead of carrying the burden of speaking in 'levels', and the connotations that come with it, Besselink argues for a shift towards a paradigm that explains the European Union as a 'polycentric' rather than a 'multilevel' polity. The European and national realm are thereby merged in a manner that goes beyond the notion of interacting levels. Concretely, as far as national parliaments are concerned, this would mean that it is quite conceivable that accountability is not only enforced as regards national governments in a purely domestic setting, but that EU institutions are taken on *as such*. That may include, for example, the demand for a justification of Council policy itself, not just of the national stance in the Council; this may furthermore include the calling to account of the European Commission in a national parliament, which is not impossible, even though commissioners are not responsible to national parliaments in a formal sense. Irrespective of the political desirability of such developments, innovative conceptualisations can and should free our mind, so that we may consider whether old paradigms are still appropriate to be applied to a new reality.

Of course, no matter how far we wish to take alternative notions of parliamentary participation and accountability in the EU, domestic ministerial responsibility to parliament will certainly remain an important link between national parliaments and EU decision-making. In that respect, two more points deserve our attention. First, we may find that sharpening domestic parliamentary scrutiny of EU matters leads to undesirable results, in that it becomes too restrictive for the government to effectively pursue European policies. It may well be attractive for a government to sometimes deliberately tie its hands, claiming that its negotiating position is rigid because its home parliament is unforgiving. After all, this adds clout to the government's bargaining stance in the Council. Yet unrestricted parliamentary supremacy, both in the field of oversight over EU policies, as well as in the field of domestic legislation with EU implications, can become highly problematic. As Siniša Rodin argues in his contribution on Croatia, the Croatian parliament keeps the government on a short leash already during the association stage with the EU. In addition, its attitude of interpreting its own legislation by means of acts of 'authentic interpretation' can very well collide with the notion that laws, and also laws implementing European law, are to be interpreted by judges, notably including the ECJ. Thus, boundless parliamentarism, which in Croatia, as Rodin argues, has its roots in pre-democratic times, may set the national parliament on a collision course with the European Union, in particular the Council, the Commission, and the ECJ, not to mention the Croatian government itself.

Another point of reflection as regards ministerial accountability would be that too strong a focus on government-parliament relations might obstruct the view on what parliamentarism should be really about, namely parliament-citizen relations. As Olaf Tans argues in his contribution on the Netherlands, it is telling that the EU Constitutional Treaty was rejected in a referendum by 61 percent of Dutch voters, whereas there was an 85 percent majority *in favour* of the Treaty in the lower chamber of the Dutch parliament. Exploring how government policy might be better embedded in parliamentary routines is thus merely one side of the coin; the other is how the elite consensus in government and parliament over Europe can be better embedded in society at large. Tying ministers to parliamentary mandates may or may not enhance the parliament's grip, and as regards direct dialogues with the EU institutions, for instance as regards subsidiarity, the Dutch parliament has in any event been surprisingly innovative in setting up a joint committee. Still it will remain a constant challenge to make sure that parliament itself is still acting on a mandate from its constituents in matters of European integration.

4 A Critical View on European Treaty-Drafting

The fact that different issues matter to different national and regional parliaments to a different extent finally brings us to a re-assessment of EU treaty-drafting practice. The Convention method of treaty revision, as applied to the Constitutional Treaty, serves two important and partly overlapping purposes: to involve national parliamentarians already in the treaty-drafting stage, and, perhaps in the process, bringing treaty-drafting closer to the citizens via openness, inclusiveness, and public deliberation. This would stand in a marked contrast with the IGC method, which is not open at all, and after which national parliaments are presented with a *fait accompli* that requires, and usually receives, their ratification, unless a referendum disrupts the procedure. Yet what have we seen with respect to the Convention on the future of Europe?

As a first point, we might note that the *content* of parliamentary participation in the Convention varied from one parliament to another. It thereby serves as a helpful reminder how heterogeneous member states, regions, and their parliaments are when it comes to their stakes in European integration. The parliament of the UK, for instance, as Adam Cygan observes, was above all keen to see that its domestic tools of enforcing ministerial responsibility are reflected at EU level as well. Thus, information facilities, as well as a formal recognition of Westminster's scrutiny reserve, whereby minister have to wait for the completion of parliamentary scrutiny at home before agreeing to EU proposals, have been high on the agenda. The Dutch parliament, meanwhile, gave high prominence to the long-term interests of the Netherlands as a whole, rather than its parliament in particular. This was, as Olaf Tans notes, expressed in an adherence to the Community method, a rotating Council presidency, and a leading role for the Commission. An upgrading of the role of the European Council was rejected, since it was perceived as consolidating the dominance of the big member states. The Scottish parliament had substantive views on its own, but, as Gordon Heggie notes, with no direct representation in the Convention, and with no say in the ratification of the Constitutional Treaty, its views had to be relayed more or less informally. The federal parliament of Belgium, meanwhile, let its representatives in the Convention deliberate basically on their own, without tying them to any mandates and without following up on their work with debates. In fact, as Wouter Pas observes, one of the representatives of the Belgian federal parliament was in fact a member of a sub-national parliament, while the other one was not a member of any parliament at all. This again goes to show that parliaments not only have diverging priorities in treaty-drafting, but that they are also very much heterogeneous in their domestic role and self-perception.

As a second point we should note that not only the direction, but also the *degree* of parliamentary participation in the Convention varied, and was in fact mostly very modest. Debates on the progress of the Convention in the parliament of the UK were limited to the interested few, namely those MPs who also usually specialise in EU matters. The Netherlands and Belgium present similar pictures, with poor or absent debates on the progress of the Convention. Thus, if the Convention was to bring Europe closer to the parliaments, it succeeded only in part, to put it mildly. That is not necessarily the Convention's fault, and it may not even be the parliaments'. For all the enthusiasm for parliamentary participation in the EU, there simply might be an inherent remoteness between Europe and the citizens, and their representatives, that simply cannot be brought down below a certain minimum.

This brings us to a third point, which is that, as already pointed out earlier, the value of parliamentarism lies not merely in the connection between parliament and government, or parliament and EU institutions, but in the link between national and European institutions, on the one hand, and the citizens, on the other hand. The added value is that citizens can engage in channelled debate, with their views finding expression in public deliberations and policy results. The Dutch case clearly shows that elite consensus over Europe does not guarantee popular consensus as to specific policy steps, and that a referendum, for that and all manner of other reasons, can be then employed to confront and embarrass the political class. Indeed, what is the value of a parliament, even a strong one, if it is united over a cause that a majority of its voters is prepared to reject?

5 Conclusion

The endorsement of national parliaments in the European Union is a cause that is at present broadly supported. Holding their ministers to account, relaying the preferences of their constituents, enforcing subsidiarity, and giving life to the notion that Europe is a polycentric entity: these are all tasks that are readily associated with parliaments. That is not to say that parliaments necessarily hold the answer to everything. Yet without them, the picture would definitely not be complete. In that context we must also take into careful consideration that, first, there is a regional dimension to national parliamentarism. Whether it concerns a question of competence allocation or subsidiarity, or substantive EU decision-making, national parliaments include regional parliaments. Sometimes, national parliament even *means* regional parliament, when the constitutional system of a member state allocates certain exclusive competences to sub-national entities, as it does in hyper-federalised Belgium. In cases where regional parliaments exist without the member state itself being federal, as in the United Kingdom, regional parliaments are called upon to define their own role by channelling their views to their own executive, or to the central national authority, but also by exploring new means of representing their constituents, such as via direct dialogues with EU institutions which bypass the national capital. Either way, regional parliaments will come to use avenues of participation that are no longer exclusively tied to classic ministerial accountability: after all, national ministers are not accountable to regional assemblies. Yet also for *national* parliaments, where such accountability does apply, there are also few formal obstacles to exploring new avenues. Restricting participation in EU matters to the process of interacting with ministers at home, who then go on and represent the member state externally, would mean to miss out on many additional points of entry to the EU policy process. Tying the ministers too much to negotiating mandates, and insisting on parliamentary supremacy both domestically and externally can, as the Croatian example shows, even produce harmful effects. Breaking free from ministerial responsibility as the sole connection to the EU would however presuppose an understanding that the EU is not a rigid hierarchical construct. In fact, it might even require to let go of the notion of 'multi-level governance' as a governing paradigm, since it still features 'levels' that appear to be mutually exclusive and otherwise independent. A 'polycentric paradigm' might open up new views on dynamic interaction between regional, national and European political protagonists.

Whatever the eventual paradigm chosen and priority taken, in all of this we should not lose sight of the fact that parliamentarism in the European Union is not merely there to connect parliaments, governments, regions, member states, and the EU institutions, but that its purpose is to connect the governing with the governed. Our judgment whether sharpening parliamentary scrutiny of governments, and expanding the notion of accountability and subsidiarity, is desirable or indeed undesirable, should always be intimately connected with the question whether such developments can be embedded, and accepted as such, in society at large.

CHAPTER 2

The EU Constitutional Treaty from the Perspective of the Parliament of the United Kingdom

An Improved Framework for Parliamentary Scrutiny?

Adam Cygan

1 Brief History of Parliamentary Scrutiny in the United Kingdom

The history and work of both the European scrutiny committee in the House of Commons and the select committee on the European Union in the House of Lords can be traced back to the mid 1970s. The work of these, and any other national parliamentary committee examining EU affairs in the UK, predates references to national parliaments in the European treaties. What is noteworthy is that the current systems in both houses still remain largely consistent with the 1973 reports which formed the initial basis for European scrutiny,[1] with many of the same problems facing the scrutiny committees today as they did thirty years ago. Procedures have inevitably been adapted in the light of experience and treaty developments, and mandates have been enlarged, but no fundamental change has taken place. Ministerial accountability for decisions taken in the EU Council of Ministers remains the priority. That said, three important recent developments should be noted.

First, the process of parliamentary scrutiny has been the subject of very detailed and critical review in both houses.[2] Such reviews were underway prior to the commencement of the Convention process but no formal changes have yet arisen as a result of the Convention or the provisions of the Constitutional Treaty. Procedures have over the years been adapted in the light of experience

1 In December 1972, both houses appointed select committees to consider what procedures should be established to scrutinise legislative proposals and other documents emanating from the European Communities. In the Commons the committee was chaired by Sir John Foster. The committee laid down the basis for scrutiny in the Commons as described below. Lord Maybray-King chaired the Lords committee. The principal recommendation of its report (1972-73, HL 194), presented in July 1973, was to set up a sessional select committee. The select committee on the European Communities was set up on 10 April 1974. It was reappointed at the beginning of each parliamentary session until it was superseded, in December 1999, by the select committee on the European Union.

2 In 1998 the scrutiny of European legislation in the Commons came under review by the select committee on modernisation of the House of Commons. Reports on the scrutiny process in the Commons were prepared in 1996 and 1997, by the select committee on European legislation (twenty-seventh report 1995-96) and the select committee on procedure (third report 1996-97), respectively. The upshot of the review was a redrawing of the terms of reference of the Commons committee, significantly by extending its remit to Second and Third Pillar matters. Its scrutiny reserve resolution (the effect of which is explained below) has also been amended to include references to texts requiring a decision of the Council of Ministers under the Second and Third Pillars. The committee was also renamed the European scrutiny committee. Shortly after those changes in the Commons, the terms of reference of the Lords scrutiny committee were revised and the Lords adopted its own scrutiny reserve resolution. This was done essentially to bring the terms of reference into line with those of the Commons committee, to reflect the extension of the scrutiny reserve to Second and Third Pillar matters, and to make clear, by adoption of its own resolution, the operation of the scrutiny reserve in the context of procedures in the House of Lords. The Lords committee was renamed the European Union committee.

and events with the terms of reference of the committees being enlarged when necessary. Both houses recognised that an approval of the Constitutional Treaty would necessitate changes to their respective scrutiny arrangements. Judging by past practice, such changes would only occur subsequent to a detailed review of procedures in the light of the Constitutional Treaty. The key development in recent years has been a more systematic review of Second and Third Pillar activities. In the House of Lords, a number of reforms were made following the select committee's review and report in 2002.[3] The reform process is continuing. One area that remains problematic for the committees is the review of decisions taken via the comitology procedure and soft law processes such as the open method of coordination, and the Convention offered little hope for improvement in respect of the review of non-Community method proposals.

Second, the UK national parliament office has been established in Brussels. This is an important point of contact between the two houses and the Union's institutions, especially the European Parliament. The office provides a valuable source of direct information for the two scrutiny committees.

Third, the modernisation committee of the House of Commons has recently proposed the establishment of a joint committee of the two houses to consider matters related to the European Union (the Parliamentary European Committee).[4] This proposal, which has been regularly discussed since the late 1980s, is considered further at the end of this contribution. The proposal was specifically linked to the debate within the Convention for improved accountability and was considered as a mechanism through which the UK parliament as a whole could provide a coherent single view to ministers on policy developments within the EU. However, the purpose of any such committee would not be to create a unitary scrutiny system in the UK parliament, with this being left to both houses to pursue according to their own procedures and requirements.

A key feature of scrutiny activities in both houses is that the task is delegated to specialist committees and sub-committees. No review of EU legislative proposals is undertaken by the specialist departmental select committees in the Commons or Lords. That is not to suggest that these committees are not interested in EU matters. They will consider legislative proposals as part of wider policy investigations which their standing orders require of them. However, the mechanics of scrutiny are left to the specialist EU committees. Though this has allowed for the development of expertise within the committees, it has relegated EU affairs from the mainstream of parliamentary activity, perhaps reinforcing an impression that EU affairs are peripheral to governmental activity. This 'tradition' continued with the participation in, and review of, Convention business taking place primarily within the specialist EU committees.

---

3 *Review of Scrutiny of European Legislation* (HL 15 first report 2002-03).

4 Select committee on modernisation of the House of Commons, second report, *Scrutiny of European Business* (HC 465 2004-05).

2 Scrutiny as Substitute Sovereignty?

After thirty years of EC/EU membership, the primary objectives for the scrutiny committees in both houses remain the *ex ante* review of EU legislative proposals and the influencing of the minister prior to his or her attending the Council. The objective of both houses within the Convention process was to improve and strengthen this role, rather than to create some new mechanism or institution to undertake the task of scrutiny. In this context the approach of the UK parliament to the Convention was to push for developments that would make internal parliamentary procedures more effective, and specifically this entailed formalising the position of national scrutiny reserves within the Council's rule of procedure.

The scrutiny reserve, which essentially bars ministers from giving their consent to EU measures pending domestic parliamentary scrutiny, has provided the UK committees with a closer monitoring function of Council decision-making, with ministers being subject to *ex post* accountability if they breach the scrutiny reserve. Through such scrutiny, the Commons and Lords are seeking to transfer to European legislative proposals those traditional constitutional principles, collectively referred to as executive accountability, which are readily apparent when reviewing domestic legislative measures. At the core of this is the requirement of government ministers to come to the despatch box and explain their actions. In this context the two houses, and perhaps the Commons more specifically, have attempted to maintain the same rigorous review of executive action in relation to European legislative proposals as are applied to domestic ones.

The form of scrutiny undertaken by the both houses can be categorised as substitute sovereignty – the more scrutiny that occurs, the more that MPs and peers may consider that this operates as a counterbalance for legislative sovereignty that has been transferred to the EU level. The goal of executive scrutiny should not be understated and the work of the committees must be considered a crucial task, as it remains to this day the only direct parliamentary control over the UK government throughout the entire EU decision-making procedure.

In 1973 the aim of both the Foster and Maybray-King committees, which were to devise scrutiny systems in connection with the UK's EEC accession, was to put forward a framework for scrutiny that would secure both houses of parliament the maximum influence over the executive. While the aim of the UK parliament within the Convention was to continue with this theme, increased EU competence and qualified majority voting have, over time, made this more difficult. An objective for the UK parliament was to seek to redress this balance shift particularly through improved subsidiarity monitoring. One issue raised within the Foster committee was that the Commons would only be able to maintain influence if legislative proposals were in the form of directives rather than regulations.[5] This misconception demonstrates not only how the perception of

[5] See HC 463-II (1972-73) paragraphs 723-725.

scrutiny within the Commons has been dominated from the outset by a desire to uphold parliamentary sovereignty, but also how political actors have over the years misunderstood the impact of European law within the UK legal system.[6]

The European scrutiny committee in the Commons has through time come to appreciate that the function it performs on behalf of the chamber is different from that which is performed when the Commons reviews domestic legislative proposals. Most significantly, the European scrutiny committee cannot propose amendments to a legislative proposal, making the directive/regulation distinction redundant with regard to the content of a proposal. In an omni-competent and enlarged EU, the task of parliamentary committees should not be to claw back sovereignty through excessive domestic scrutiny which ultimately has minimal impact within the Council. Rather, given that the objective of scrutiny is to influence the minister *ex ante*, scrutiny procedures should be seeking to employ effective and targeted mechanisms to achieve this very objective. Therefore the need for functioning scrutiny reserves is the primary conclusion that emanated from the Convention's working group IV, which dealt with the role of national parliaments in the EU, as a fundamental and common principle to which all national parliaments can adhere, irrespective of their individual domestic scrutiny arrangements.

Both houses in the UK have made it clear in the Convention that some form of new EU institution representing national parliaments at the EU level and performing this scrutiny function is not required.[7] However, the difficulty facing all national parliaments lies in the fact that it is the progress of the decision-making process itself that ultimately governs when, and to what extent, such scrutiny will occur. The present lack of co-ordination between the EU institutions and domestic parliaments over issues such as the legislative timetable, or the lack of sufficient time for scrutiny, goes to the heart of the unease that exists in the relationship between them.[8] This, in part, is one explanation why, in the past, the Commons has compensated for the transfer of competence with over-rigorous scrutiny. For the House of Commons, problems of transparency and efficient provision of documentation with their roots firmly in the EU

---

6 Evidenced clearly through the *Factortame* litigation and the UK's failure to appreciate the impact of the Merchant Shipping Act 1988 on the rights contained in Article 43 EC.

7 See HL 48 (2001-2) *A Second Parliamentary Chamber for the EU: an Unreal Solution to some Real Problems* and HC 152 xxxiii-I (2001-2) *Democracy and Accountability in the EU and the Role of National Parliaments.*

8 Though in his statement of 11 February 2004, the foreign secretary stated that from April 2004, and then subsequently every January, the government will seek to aid the committee in its task by laying before the house a white paper looking at the year ahead for the EU's legislative and other activities. The objective of the paper will be to set out the government's priorities in the light of the Commission's legislative and work programme for the year ahead, as well as the operational programme for the forthcoming EU presidencies agreed each December by the European Council. See HC Debs. 11 February 2004, Col. 1416.

are directly linked to the operation of scrutiny reserves. In its submission to the Convention, the committee concluded that these issues must first be addressed before any progress can be made to resolve the wider problem of direct disconnection between the EU institutions and citizens.[9]

Scrutiny remains effective if it is pre-legislative and based upon the timely provision of all available documentation. The committees seek to achieve this through enforcing the scrutiny reserve which reinforces the argument that parliamentary scrutiny procedures amount to substitute sovereignty. The reserve, which seeks to maximise executive accountability, is primarily intended for domestic parliamentary consumption to reassure sceptical MPs that the views of the UK parliament do matter and are relevant to EU decision-making. Consequently, the introspective nature of the reserve leads it to operate independently of the Council timetable. Working group IV recognised that this is unsatisfactory and that scrutiny reserves require greater prominence in the European treaties if national parliaments are themselves to believe they have not become peripheral to the process of European integration. The Constitutional Treaty protocols and related provisions would go part of the way, at least, to addressing this.

Connected to these arguments of substitute sovereignty is the fundamental question of which level of governance should have competence to legislate in a given policy area. The House of Commons in its submission to the Convention highlighted that it would like to see more subsidiarity in practice as decision-making at the national level suggests increased executive accountability. Through the transfer of competence to the EU level, the view is reinforced that domestic scrutiny compensates for the loss of actual legislative sovereignty. Both committees have, to this end, made it clear that they would need to review their existing procedures in the light of the Constitutional Treaty provisions relating to national parliaments to ensure that ministerial accountability is maintained and, when possible, enhanced.

3 Scrutiny of European Union Legislation by the Westminster Parliament

The work of the two EU select committees has as its core two *essential* common features. These are (a) the deposit of EU documents and accompanying explanatory memoranda; and (b) the scrutiny reserve resolution. Information remains central to effective scrutiny and both committees use internal parliamentary procedures to ensure a consistent and efficient flow of information. In this context, the primary target of the committees is Her Majesty's Government. However, if documentation is delayed from Brussels this can seriously inhibit the opportunity for effective scrutiny and no amount

9 See HC 63-xxiv (2003-03) p. 7, paragraph 8.

of internal reform to parliamentary procedure can compensate for this. In both houses, EU matters are delegated to specific committees who undertake scrutiny activities on behalf of the whole house. This delegation to a specialist committee undoubtedly makes the scrutiny process more efficient and effective.

3.1 European Union Documents

The two committees scrutinise 'European Union documents'.[10] The term is given a broad meaning and covers proposals for Community legislation and a large variety of other documents issuing under the treaties. They include the Commission's annual work programme, green and white papers, reports and communications, reports of the Court of Auditors and, importantly, Second and Third Pillar documents (draft common strategies, joint actions or common positions in the former case and draft common positions, framework decisions, decisions or conventions in the latter case).[11] When in the course of legislation a new text is produced, such as an amended Commission proposal or a Council common position, a new document is thereby generated and the scrutiny process begins again.[12]

EU documents are deposited in parliament by the foreign and Commonwealth office, which is the lead department for EU affairs, within two working days of their receipt in London. Within ten days of deposit the lead sectoral department is expected to provide an explanatory memorandum to the committees signed by a minister. As a public document it is the minister's evidence to parliament and is the start of the ministerial accountability process.

The requirement to provide an explanatory memorandum is an important and valuable feature of the system. It enables the two scrutiny committees to assess the documents quickly and it establishes at the outset the constitutional imperative of scrutiny, namely the accountability of ministers to parliament and its committees for their conduct with regard to those documents.

---

10 This term is defined in the House of Commons standing order no. 143. The definition is reproduced, in identical terms, in the motion appointing the House of Lords committee, which is renewed at the start of each parliamentary session.

11 Second and Third Pillar documents were brought within the terms of reference of the Commons committee as a result of the 1998 recommendations of the modernisation committee.

12 A practical example of this can be seen in the scrutiny of the draft directive on minimum standards for granting and withdrawing refugee status in member states. The publication and debate of the European Union committee's report, *Minimum Standards in Asylum Procedures* (HL 59 eleventh report 2000-01) was not the end of the story by any means. Subsequent versions of the directive or of particular Articles were furnished to the committees for scrutiny. Each was subjected to a rigorous critical examination by sub-committee E (law and institutions).

3.2 The Scrutiny Reserve Resolution

The cornerstone of the UK system of scrutiny is the scrutiny reserve resolution. Both houses share the same resolution.[13] The key point is that the resolution restricts the freedom of ministers to give agreement to a legislative proposal in Council until parliamentary scrutiny is completed. The resolution provides that no minister of the Crown shall give agreement to any proposal for European Community legislation, or for one of the specific instruments of title V or title VI of the Treaty on European Union, which is still subject to parliamentary scrutiny. In practice this means proposals or instruments on which the scrutiny committee has not completed its scrutiny, or which is awaiting consideration by the house in that it has been recommended for debate and the debate has not yet taken place. The resolution has a saving for any proposal which is 'confidential, routine or trivial, or is substantially the same as a proposal on which scrutiny has been completed'. The minister may also give agreement to a proposal still subject to scrutiny 'if he decides that for special reasons agreement should be given'. In such circumstances the minister is required to explain his or her reasons to the committee or the house at the first opportunity. However such an explanation will by its very nature always be *ex post* and this remains the weak link in the chain of ministerial accountability.

It has been contended that ministers are increasingly reluctant to override the scrutiny reserve.[14] Certainly there is much more transparency about the process of overriding scrutiny. The government or cabinet office now provides the scrutiny committees with statistical information about how many times scrutiny has been overridden. This information is published in the committees' annual reports. In 2004, the scrutiny reserve resolution was overridden on 38 occasions, 16 in the first six months and 22 in the second. Scrutiny overrides are a matter to which both committees pay careful attention and a minister may be called to give evidence to explain the need to override the scrutiny reserve.[15]

4 Impact of the Scrutiny Process in the UK

It is difficult to assess what effect parliamentary scrutiny has in practice, and perhaps only ministers and civil servants can give a meaningful answer to that question. However, three observations may be offered regard-

---

[13] Resolution of the House of Commons of 17 November 1998 modifying the resolution of 24 October 1990, which replaced a 1980 resolution, which in turn replaced successive ministerial undertakings to a similar effect. Resolution of the House of Lords of 6 December 1999.

[14] See Digby Jones, *UK Parliamentary Scrutiny of EU Legislation*, The Foreign Policy Centre, April 2005, p. 5.

[15] House of Commons European scrutiny committee, *The work of the Committee in 2004* (sixth report 2004-05) at par. 14.

ing the work of both select committees within the UK parliament. First, the discipline required of ministers when having to submit explanatory memoranda and to respond, in writing and sometimes in person, to questions raised by the scrutiny committees, should not be dismissed. This is a more subtle form of ministerial accountability. There can be little doubt that it is an important and efficient means of keeping the government of the day accountable to parliament. Though, as mentioned, there have been a substantial number of occasions when the scrutiny reserve has been overridden by the government, it remains a real and effective check on ministers. In particular the requirement that they must explain their actions in public ensures that any decision to bypass parliament is not taken lightly. In this context ministers cannot rely on the support of their own party members who are appointed to the committees. In the Commons, though the composition of the committee is in proportion to the number of MPs elected and thus favours the party in government, the committee tends to act with a high degree of collegiality and consensus, and this is also the case in the House of Lords. This behaviour reinforces the constitutional convention of ministerial accountability which in such circumstances the committee secures on behalf of parliament. Such a consensus is an undoubted strength, and one which is generally lacking within the chamber of the House of Commons itself where adversarial politics are the norm.

Second, parliamentary scrutiny can contribute substantially to the transparency and openness of the European Union's legislative process and arguably help to aid citizen understanding of EU activities. Perhaps the best examples of this can be seen in the scrutiny of Third Pillar measures. The House of Lords' work on Europol is a good instance of bringing to the wider attention of both parliament and the media the development of policy under the Third Pillar. The select committee has issued a number of reports concerning the European police office.[16] The first report on Europol, published in 1995, examined the underlying convention in draft form. The later reports considered some of the detailed rules and regulations made under the convention, those on the confidentiality regulations and the joint supervisory body, taking further the interests identified in the first report (especially the need to monitor the exchange of personal data and to protect individual rights) and, significantly, placing in the public domain the details of the rule-making under the convention. A later report, published in 2003, assessed Europol's role in fighting crime and made a number of recommendations relating to its remit and practices.[17] Most recently, Europol was one of a number of bodies whose work was assessed by the committee in its report on the EU's response to terrorism.[18]

---

16 *EUROPOL* (HL 51 tenth report 1994-95); *EUROPOL: Confidentiality Regulations* (HL 9 first report 1997-98); *EUROPOL: Joint Supervisory Body* (HL 71 thirteenth report 1997-98); *EUROPOL: Third Country Rules* (HL 135 twenty-ninth report 1997-98).

17 *Europol's Role in Fighting Crime* (HL 43 fifth report 2002-03).

18 *After Madrid: the EU's respose to terrorism* (HL 53 fifth report 2004-05).

Third, the work of the scrutiny committees can have a direct impact on the progress or content of legislation. It is frequently said that Commission officials read House of Lords reports assiduously. Whether or not that is true, there have been instances where the select committee's recommendations have led to change in the measure being negotiated. An example can be seen in the 1999 Council decision on procedures regarding the Commission's comitology.[19] At the outset of its inquiry into the (then) draft decision, the committee asked to be supplied with a complete list of comitology committees. The Community institutions contended that this was not possible, but the fact that the select committee required, and the UK government actually produced a list showed that it was not impossible, and the select committee's recommendation that there should be a published list of comitology committees was taken into the final text of the decision.[20] Despite this it remains very difficult to measure accurately circumstances where committee reports lead to direct changes in legislative proposals.

5 The United Kingdom Parliament and the Convention Process

It would not be inaccurate to suggest that the Convention process generated only a minimal impact upon the work of the UK parliament. In the UK parliament it is the domestic legislative agenda which dominates parliamentary business. Furthermore, in the current UK political climate, in which the process of EU integration raises numerous difficulties for both government and opposition parties, debating the Convention in public in an election year was avoided. This led to debate about the progress of the Convention being, in the main, confined to the EU committees of both houses and the foreign affairs select committee in the House of Commons. All the major political parties appointed representatives to the Convention but the public impact of their contributions failed to attract any significant attention in the media. From a UK perspective it would be fair to suggest that the work of the Convention and the debate it generated was confined primarily to parliamentarians who usually participate in the review of EU affairs.

Working group IV of the Convention on the future of Europe provided the primary forum in which the future role of national parliaments was discussed. From the UK parliament both houses, through their European scrutiny committees, made submissions to the working group which highlighted two major points which related to the exercise of domestic scrutiny. The first concerned the need to provide extra time for scrutiny, more than is provided for in the Amsterdam protocol on the role of national parliaments, for review of amendments

[19] Council decision 1999/468/EC of 28 June 1999 laying down the procedures for the exercise of implementing powers conferred on the Commission, [1999] OJ L184/23.

[20] *Delegation of powers to the Commission: Reforming Comitology* (third Report 1998-99).

proposed by the European Parliament under co-decision. Specifically this related to the prompt provision of all documentation to enable the domestic scrutiny task to be fulfilled, and central to this is giving a clearer status to scrutiny reserves in the Council's rules of procedure. Secondly, both committees recognised that the primary role for national parliaments was to be involved in the *ex ante* monitoring of subsidiarity, which as a political concept, they concluded, was particularly suited to the functions of parliamentary institutions.

Generally, the input to the Convention varied across the national parliaments. It is perhaps unsurprising that for the United Kingdom parliament the emphasis was placed upon securing accountability of ministers and ensuring adequate time for scrutiny through some clearer status of scrutiny reserves. Together these two issues are central to the constitutional doctrine of ministerial accountability to parliament. This parliament-versus-government type of scrutiny is a feature of the majoritarian government that exists within the UK. It was therefore not unexpected that the House of Commons in its submission to the Convention[21] referred to the UK scrutiny reserve as the 'cornerstone' of its scrutiny activities and as one which must have greater prominence within the Council.

Within the overall context of monitoring subsidiarity, the objective of the UK parliament was to improve the political accountability of the minister. Subsidiarity, as working group I of the Convention concluded, is a political concept and is most appropriate for review by national parliaments in the light of the EU's multi-level governance structure. The subsidiarity protocol is intended to provide a degree of commonality between national parliaments in relation to their scrutiny activities.[22] While scrutiny procedures and constitutional traditions may differ across twenty-five national parliaments, the objective of securing relevant, concise and above all *intra vires* EU legislation permeates across all national parliaments. Consequently the Constitutional Treaty protocol on the application of subsidiarity and the subsidiarity early warning mechanism in Article I-11 of the Constitutional Treaty are broadly welcomed by the United Kingdom parliament, and were perhaps viewed as being more significant than the protocol on national parliaments.[23] This is because, in relation to scrutiny issues and provision of documentation to parliament, both committees tend to have established a reasonably good co-operation with the government and the framework of the scrutiny reserve provides for a business-like working relation-

[21] See HC 152 xxxiii-I (2001-2) at 7 above.

[22] See HL Paper 70 (2002-03) *The Future of Europe: National Parliaments and Subsidiarity – the Proposed Protocols.*

[23] Though a proposal to the Convention for a 'red card' procedure which would give national parliaments a veto over a legislative proposal was rejected. It was proposed by Gisela Stuart MP to the House of Lords select committee on the European Union, HL 70 (2002-03) *The Future of Europe: National Parliaments and Subsidiarity – The Proposed Protocols*, QQ 6-10.

ship, though there are undoubtedly occasions when adequate information will not be received by the committees.[24]

The UK parliament has, since the concept was first introduced in the Maastricht Treaty, demonstrated enthusiasm with monitoring and enforcing subsidiarity. In some respects this comes back to the concept of parliamentary sovereignty and is viewed by the UK parliament as having some degree of influence over the EU legislative process. Though the UK parliament takes the task of competence monitoring very seriously, it may overestimate the amount of influence it can exercise over the executive. While the United Kingdom parliament may be considered as a (modest) policy-making legislature within a domestic context, it is not able to effectively alter a governmental draft reaction to an EU policy initiative. Though parliament and minister may differ on the question of subsidiarity, it would be, perhaps, overstating parliament's influence to suggest that it can regularly alter the minister's opinion in relation to the most appropriate level of governance to introduce the legislative proposal. The UK system of scrutiny, which is very much document-based, uses explanatory texts produced by the government as the basis for deciding competence issues. These focused government 'translations' of EU information are of high political relevance, since they allow MPs not only to discuss the documents as such, but also the government's perspective on a given issue. In these circumstances, it is very hard for parliament, with the limited time available, to alter the minister's opinion, though that is not to suggest that it will not try and is precisely why parliament gave such prominence to the issues of scrutiny reserves and provision of information within the Convention.

Closely allied to subsidiarity and competence issues is the question of how new policy fields and new modes of governance evade any parliamentary guidance or control. Together with the issue of comitology, these developments were highlighted by both houses as not being subject to rigorous and systematic scrutiny. Some of these fields have evolved recently, e.g. foreign policy and common security, justice and home affairs, economic and monetary policy in the context of the EMU, the euro area countries' policies within the framework of the growth and stability pact, and the so-called 'open method of co-ordination' policies. In these areas both the Amsterdam and the Nice Treaty reforms have not made any progress towards an inclusion of at least one level of parliamentary participation, whilst they have sanctioned particularly innovative decisions at strictly intergovernmental level, such as those concerning the introduction of a political and military structure for common crisis reaction forces or the setting up of new intergovernmental committees in the fields of EMU and employment.

New modes of governance have therefore created new democratic deficits at both levels. The recent tendency to replace the Community method of decision-making became obvious with the decision of the heads of state and government on the European security and defence policy, where the intergovernmental

---

[24] Ibid.

dimension in steering the Union had been strengthened, as expressed most clearly in the emphasis given to the role of the European Council. The key issues of transparency in relation to tracing and monitoring the Council's activities were merely touched upon in a few provisions of the Amsterdam Treaty, and have left national parliaments as bystanders. Addressing this problem through the Convention was an important issue for the United Kingdom parliament which recognised that policy coordination would become increasingly prominent in an EU of twenty-five member states. For the United Kingdom parliament, the view was taken that the same rules of adequate and efficient provision of documentation and sufficient time for discussion should apply to these new policy-making processes.

6 The UK Parliament after the Convention

The European scrutiny process in the United Kingdom has recently come under criticism, notably for the lack of awareness of MPs and, more generally, the public, about legislative proposals emanating from Brussels.[25] The good work of the two scrutiny committees has been acknowledged but there remains, it is strongly argued by the government and such bodies as the CBI, an employers' lobby, a failure of MPs to engage with and in the European legislative process. One solution promoted in the last parliament was the creation of a joint grand committee for Europe.[26] It is envisaged that the committee would meet about four times a year, two of which would be devoted to considering the foreign secretary's six-monthly white papers on Europe. MEPs would be allowed to attend. Commissioners and Commission officials might also participate in meetings of the new committee but, the report makes clear, would not be subject to scrutiny by the joint committee. Their role would be to share information, to inform the debate and to foster dialogue between the Commission and the UK parliament. What seems clear is that the new joint committee would not take over or displace the regular detailed scrutiny work undertaken by the two scrutiny committees. The CBI has commented: 'clearly such an infrequently-meeting committee could not launch an inquiry, or examine an issue in any detail, and thus would not contribute significantly to the scrutiny process'.[27] Such criticisms deserve careful examination. For example, the joint committee might well have to be selective, but one cannot rule out the possibility that at a well-prepared meeting it might examine a minister or Commissioner on a particular proposal (e.g. the controversial services directive) in some detail. How it might strengthen parliamentary awareness and scrutiny

---

25 See Digby Jones, footnote 14 *supra*, p. 5.

26 Select committee on modernisation of the House of Commons, second report, *Scrutiny of European Business* (HC 465 2004-05).

27 See Digby Jones, footnote 14 *supra*, p. 6.

of European legislation and policies is to be seen. Whether, and how best, the grand committee might complement and supplement the detailed work of the scrutiny committees needs further consideration.

Any future development in relation to the work and practical arrangements of both committees in response to the Constitutional Treaty remains on hold during the EU's 'pause for reflection'. In practice this will require that national parliaments must wait and see what, if any, parts of the Treaty may be salvaged. The provisions of the Constitutional Treaty which relate to national parliaments would improve their ability to conduct scrutiny and arguably could be introduced without the need for a specific treaty, and there are good arguments for doing so. Most importantly for national parliaments, the changes should improve the status of scrutiny reserves in the Council and promote improved access to documentation. Such changes could be introduced through an amendment to the Council's rules of procedure, and by the Commission making documents available more efficiently. Such piecemeal implementation of the Treaty is not favoured, least of all by national parliaments, and is unlikely to occur. That said, such reform would assist committees, such as those in the UK parliament, to ensure ministerial accountability is upheld, EU legislation is more transparent, and that ultimately citizens are better informed of their rights and obligations. As long as the future position of national parliaments is tied up so closely with the fate of the Constitutional Treaty, it is unlikely that progress will be made to address these deficits.

CHAPTER 3

The Scottish Parliament and the EU Constitution

Moving Beyond the Principle of Partnership?

Gordon Heggie

1 Introduction

The Scottish parliament had no formal role in the process to negotiate and ratify the Treaty establishing a Constitution for Europe. There was no Scottish parliamentary representation on the Convention on the future of Europe, and the assent of the Scottish parliament will not be required to ratify the Treaty. The key question therefore, that this contribution will seek to address, is how and to what extent did the Scottish parliament participate in and influence this debate?

In evidence to the Scottish parliament's European and external relations committee, the then UK minister for Europe Peter Hain provided an insight into how the Scottish parliament could influence the debate on the future of Europe. The expectations were that 'the principal vehicle' for Scottish input was to be the UK government. As he went on to discuss the 'principle' that would 'govern the political relationship' between the UK government, the Scottish executive and the Scottish parliament, he referred to it as one of 'partnership'.[1] Assessing the operation of this 'principle of partnership' will be an important aspect in examining the role of the Scottish parliament in negotiating and ratifying the Treaty establishing a Constitution for Europe. The first section of this contribution will therefore seek to develop a fuller understanding of what is meant by the 'principle of partnership'. The starting point for this analysis will be to highlight the extent to which 'partnerships' are important in the relationship that exists between sub-national, national and supranational actors within EU decision-making. This section will also include a brief parliamentary history of the 'principle of partnership' by examining aspects of the relationship that has developed between the Scottish parliament, the Scottish executive, the UK government and the European Union.

Despite relations with the EU being reserved to the UK parliament and government after devolution, the expectations were that the creation of the Scottish parliament would provide a number of new opportunities for 'Scotland to contribute both reactively and proactively to the European Union'.[2] In particular, it was envisaged that these new opportunities would enable the parliament to influence EU policy 'both directly and through the United Kingdom channels'.[3] Thus, whilst developing partnerships with the UK government was important in allowing the Scottish parliament to participate in the Treaty process, this was never going to be the sole route of participation. The second section of this contribution will therefore seek to broaden the analysis by assessing the extent to which the Scottish parliament moved beyond the 'principle of partnership'. Particular focus will be placed upon the activities of the parliament's European and external relations committee, which since 1999 has provided the main parliamentary forum for debate on EU-related issues.

---

1 European and External Relations Committee, Official Report, 5 November 2001: Col 1280.

2 Scottish Office (1998) par. 8.

3 European and External Relations Committee, Official Report, 23 June 1999: Col 3.

With no separate Scottish bill required to ratify the Constitutional Treaty, Scottish parliamentary scrutiny of the UK government's European Union bill takes on extra significance. The third section will provide an examination of this process. The EU bill has two main purposes. The first was to enable the EU Constitutional Treaty to have legal effect in the UK, whilst the second was to provide for a referendum to approve the Treaty. Important in the analysis of this piece of legislation will be to examine how the proposed subsidiarity mechanisms will operate. Early discussions suggest that some form of formal mechanisms will be established to ensure Scottish parliamentary involvement. This contribution will assess these proposed mechanisms and question whether they will be sufficient to allow the Scottish parliament to participate in, and influence, decisions made in relation to subsidiarity.

2 Sub-National Parliaments, Partnerships and Multi-Level Governance

The concept of multi-level governance develops a number of propositions that help understand the development of a decision-making process that increasingly began to 'engage the activities of sub national, national and supranational agencies, institutions and non-governmental organisations'.[4] The result has been for decision-making to become 'structured around informal contacts, networks and norms, and no longer involves clear hierarchies of power and competences'.[5] In explaining the 'multi-actorness'6 of the EU's decision-making process, multi-level governance emphasises the existence of partnerships, power sharing and interdependence across and between multiple levels of government. Whilst not denying the importance of the role still played by national governments, an inevitable consequence of moves towards closer European integration has been a dilution of their power. The EU provides a striking illustration of an organisation whose decision-making procedures are primarily characterised by the 'existence of overlapping competences among multiple levels of governments and the interaction of political actors across those levels. Member state executives, while powerful, are only one set among a variety of actors in the European polity'.[7]

A consequence of the emergence of a multi-level Europe has been the increased scope for sub-national actors to pursue extra-state relations.[8] Through a combination of direct participation in EU institutions, the setting up of regional offices in Brussels, and the establishment of transnational networks,

4 Judge and Earnshaw (2003) 21.

5 Ibid.

6 Rosamond (2000) 111.

7 See Marks et al. (1996) 41.

8 See Jeffery (1997).

sub-national interests have been able to 'mobilize directly in the European arena'.[9] The multi-level governance literature notes that being able to exploit these 'channels of access' to EU decision-making has allowed sub-national governments in particular to become pro-active in influencing decisions.

The prime example of the role sub-national governments have developed within the EU's policy processes are the links established with the European Commission. Studies of multi-level governance stress the importance of a Commission-region relationship, which is portrayed as evidence of the institutionalisation of 'partnerships' between the sub-national and supranational levels. The key moment for the development of these 'partnerships' was the reform of structural fund policy, which heralded a new era of multi-level decision-making within the EU. However, when the analytical focus is redirected from specific 'policy areas' to an 'institution' then a different interpretation of the links between the sub-national level and the European Commission can be developed. In the case of the Scottish parliament, the links established between its European and external relations committee and the Commission were of an informal nature, which are restricted to annual visits to Brussels and discussions with Commission officials based in Edinburgh. This relationship is in stark contrast to the institutionalised partnerships that are prominent within existing accounts of multi-level governance.

3 The 'Principle of Partnership' in Operation

In discussing how the partnership between the Scottish parliament, the Scottish executive and the UK government would operate, Peter Hain cited the European and external relations committee's report on fisheries as 'a practical win for partnership'.[10] As Peter Hain went on to discuss, the conclusions contained within this report enabled the Scottish executive to 'significantly influence the negotiating stance adopted by the UK Government in the Council of Ministers'.[11] However, it is also possible to use the same example to highlight specific problems with the 'principle of partnership.'

One critic of the relationship between the Scottish executive and the UK government was European and external relations committee member Colin Campbell of the Scottish National Party. In the official report Mr Campbell highlighted a specific instance which he felt typified the problem of transparency. The problem stemmed from a series of questions he tabled to the then deputy minister for environment and rural development, Rhona Brankin of the Labour Party, in order to discover whom the minister had spoken to regarding the presentation of Scotland's case to the UK and Europe in relation to the

---

9 Hooghe and Marks (2001) 24.

10 European and External Relations Committee, Official Report, 5 November 2001: Col 1285.

11 European and External Relations Committee, Official Report, 5 November 2001: Col 1275.

common fisheries policy. His main complaint was that the attitude he encountered was uncooperative:

> To tell you whom we spoke to six months ago might make it more difficult for us to have confidential discussions in the future between the Scottish Executive and the UK about matters pertaining to Europe. Frankly, that is mince. It does not stand up in terms of democratic accountability. I am not looking for secrets; I wish to know the history of the meeting.[12]

The example of fisheries policy is perhaps not the best illustration of the 'principle of partnership' in operation. Whilst it can be argued that fisheries policy is a prime example of the influence the Scottish executive can exert upon the negotiating position of the UK government, it is also an example of a lack of transparency that exists in the parliament-executive relationship. If the process to negotiate and ratify the EU Constitutional Treaty was to be based upon a 'principle of partnership' as envisaged by Peter Hain, then it is essential that the relationship between the Scottish parliament and the Scottish executive be based predominantly upon transparency.

4 Moving Beyond the 'Principle of Partnership'?

During a parliamentary debate on the European Constitutional Treaty, the former convenor of the European and external relations committee, Irene Oldfather from the Labour Party, poured scorn on those who questioned the extent of Scottish parliamentary involvement in the Convention on the future of Europe. She argued that the Constitutional Treaty had been the subject of 'more consultation' than any other 'treaty revision in the history of the European Union'.[13] Not only had the committee:

> deliberated on the matter for about a year and a half, but we produced a report that was welcomed by the President of the European Parliament and 90 per cent of which was adopted in the UK submission to the European convention. We also made joint submissions with the network of regional parliamentary European Committees.[14]

Since 1999 the European and external relations committee has provided the main parliamentary forum for debate and discussion on EU matters. In relation to the EU Constitutional Treaty the committee produced two relevant reports. The first of these was a report published in December 2001 on the *Governance*

[12] European and External Relations Committee, Official Report, 22 November 2001: Col 1189.

[13] Scottish Parliament Official Record 29 April 2004: Col 7890.

[14] Scottish Parliament Official Record 29 April 2004: Col 7889.

of the European Union and the Future of Europe. This report was the result of a seven-month inquiry that accumulated evidence from a number of sources including the UK minister for Europe, members of the House of Commons, members of the European Parliament, members of the Committee of the Regions and a number of civic organisations within Scotland.

A key objective for this report was 'to initiate debate in Scotland on how the European Union should be governed and what the role should be for Scotland'.[15] In relation to the future of Europe debate, the report made a number of specific recommendations, which the executive agreed would form the basis of their discussions with the UK government. Thus, the views and opinions of the Scottish parliament on issues such as the simplification of the EU treaties, the reform of the existing EU structure to allow for more effective decision-making, better standards for the information flow between the EU institutions and national and sub-national parliaments, the pre-legislative consultation between the Commission and constitutional regions or nations and mechanisms that would enforce the principle of subsidiarity, were all considered to be influential in the eventual position adopted by the Scottish executive.

The publication of the committee's *Report on the Future of Europe* was an attempt to influence not only the Scottish executive and the UK government, but also a wider audience. The conclusions drawn in this particular report were subsequently 'sent to ministers in both the Scottish Executive and UK Governments, members of the EU's Constitutional Convention, Scotland's MEPs and national/regional parliaments across the EU'.[16] The *Future of Europe* report included evidence gathered from the Scottish parliamentary convention on the future of Europe. Participants in this particular forum included 'politicians from all parties and within all spheres of government, along with bodies and individuals representing civic Scotland and with members of the general public'.[17] The European and external relations committee's *Report on the Future of Europe* differed from the *Governance* report in the sense that it did not provide any specific recommendations. Instead, the committee presented its views on a number of issues. In its response, the Scottish executive addressed six of these issues, agreeing with the committee's views on four and rejecting two.[18] The first view that the executive rejected referred to the committee's request for the European charter of fundamental rights to be incorporated in a future EU constitution. On this point the executive rejected the committee's view on the grounds that the present EU charter was unsuitable to be a legally binding text. The second rejection centred on the committee's desire to ensure that regions with legislative powers would have the right of direct access to the European Court of Justice. Despite these rejections, the committee noted that the execu-

15 Scottish Parliament (2001) par. 5.

16 Scottish Parliament (2002b) par. 9.

17 Ibid., par. 7.

18 Scottish Parliament (2003a).

tive's response was 'positive and generally helpful'. As the then deputy convenor, John Home Robertson, went on to point out, the fact that 'many of the ideas in the Executive's joint submission to the convention are now identifiable in the drafts of the protocols on national parliaments and the proposed early warning system to monitor subsidiarity' demonstrates that the committee has 'achieved something'.[19]

5 The Trans-European Network of Regional Parliamentary European Committees (NORPEC)

Along with its counterparts in the Flemish and Catalan parliaments, the Scottish European and external relations committee has been at the forefront of the proposals to establish the trans-European network of regional parliamentary European committees (NORPEC). This initiative was designed to build upon the links already established with other regions and to provide an 'informal network of similar Committees at the regional or sub-Member State level within the EU' and was 'specifically aimed at those legislatures with substantial legislative powers and an interest/responsibility for EU issues'.[20]

The roots of the decision to establish NORPEC can be traced to the rejection of the committee's request to join COSAC, the conference of European affairs committees of the national parliaments in the EU, as an observer. Although this request was rejected as a result of the membership of COSAC being restricted to member states, and their national parliaments, the committee decided to pursue this issue. The subsequent meetings and video-conference held between the committees of the Scottish, Flemish and Catalan parliaments agreed in principle 'to work towards the establishment of a new network of European Affairs Committees within the Regions of the EU'.[21] Whilst the Flemish committee no longer participates in NORPEC, the Scottish and Catalan committees have been joined by representatives from the Basque and Saxony-Anhalt parliaments.

Central to the thinking behind the idea of NORPEC was that at the very least it should provide a forum in which parliamentarians at the regional or subnational level could exchange ideas and share information. Indeed, NORPEC provided the Scottish parliament with a further route to participate in the Convention on the future of Europe. Along with the European affairs committee of the Catalan parliament, the Scottish European and external relations committee provided the Convention with a joint submission on regional issues. Although not officially under the auspices of NORPEC, the report presented by the Scottish committee had the full backing of its counterpart in the Catalan

19 European and External Relations Committee, Official Report, 4 March 2003: Col 1955.

20 Scottish Parliament (2002a) par. 6.

21 Ibid., Annex A.

parliament, and featured in the plenary debate on regional issues undertaken by the European Convention.

6 The European Union Bill and Scottish Parliamentary Scrutiny

The European Union bill, first introduced at Westminster on 25 January 2005, has two main objectives. The first is to amend the European Communities Act (1972) in order for the European Constitutional Treaty to have legal effect within the UK, whilst the second was to provide legislation for a referendum to approve the Constitutional Treaty. The bill received a second reading in the House of Commons on 9 February, however it was unable to proceed as a result of the subsequent general elections. Consequently, the European Union bill was re-introduced on 24 May 2005.

The rejection of the proposed Constitutional Treaty by the voters of the Netherlands and France had somewhat stifled debate within the UK. Following the outcome of these referendums, Tony Blair called for a period of reflection in which to re-consider the future of Europe. One consequence of this was the announcement by the UK government on 6 June 2005 that it was suspending the European Union bill, thus postponing its second reading.

Despite its questionable future, the European Union bill has important implications for Scotland and the Scottish parliament. It was proposed that this particular legislation be the subject of a Sewel motion, thus there would be no separate Scottish bill. The Sewel convention, named after the former minister of state in the Scottish Office, Lord Sewel, enables the UK parliament to legislate on behalf of the Scottish parliament. Sewel operates on the premise that if the:

> UK Government and the Scottish Executive agree that it is appropriate to include in a Westminster Bill provisions affecting devolved matters, the Executive invites the Parliament to give consent to those provisions being dealt with by Westminster.[22]

The obvious consequence of the European Union bill being the subject of a Sewel motion was that the assent of the Scottish parliament would not be required, thus denying the parliament the opportunity to scrutinise the legislation and debate its content. To date, scrutiny of the EU bill has been undertaken by the European and external affairs comittee. This session took place on 22 March 2005, lasted for 36 minutes, and provided the membership of the committee with the opportunity to question Tom McCabe, the Scottish Labour minister for finance and public sector reform, as well as officials from the Scottish executive.

---

[22] Scottish Parliament (2005) 1.

7 The EU Bill and Subsidiarity

In the context of EU policy-making, the principle of subsidiarity 'is a political device for managing a system of multi-tiered governance... when competence is deemed to be shared across different levels of governance'.[23] Essentially subsidiarity 'has been taken to mean that policies should be decided at the national level, and perhaps even at the regional or local levels, whenever possible'.[24] The Constitutional Treaty aims to extend the use of subsidiarity. Thus, 'although the role of sub-national/sub-state or regional actors in this process is given no formal standing' the expectation is that 'regional and local governments and parliaments will be involved in the subsidiarity dialogue'.[25]

The 'early warning system' outlined in Article 6 of the protocol on the application of the principles of subsidiarity and proportionality provides the national parliaments of the member states with the right to provide 'a reasoned opinion' why in their view an EU legislative proposal fails to 'comply with the principle of subsidiarity'. These 'reasoned opinions' must be transmitted to the presidents of the European Parliament, the Council and the Commission within a six-week timeframe. The UK government's interpretation of Article 6 was outlined in clause 3 (2) of the EU bill, which states:

> before the end of six weeks from the date of transmission, the responsible Minister must lay before Parliament a statement about whether, in his opinion, the draft legislative act complies with the principle of subsidiarity.

In relation to Article 6, the particular area of interest for the Scottish parliament concerns the suggestion that it would be 'for each national Parliament or each chamber of a national Parliament to consult, where appropriate, regional parliaments with legislative powers.' This issue represented the main line of questioning taken by the then convenor of the European and external relations committee John Swinney of the Scottish National Party. His main criticisms centred upon whether the subsidiarity mechanisms as set out in both the EU Constitutional Treaty and the government's EU bill were robust enough to ensure that the UK parliament met its obligation in consulting with the Scottish parliament. As he argued, both the Treaty and the bill did 'not read as though it were placing an express obligation on national Parliaments', instead the Article 'reads more as if it were presenting an opportunity of giving advice'.[26] Addressing his concern, Scottish minister for finance and public sector reform, Tom McCabe stressed that the

---

23 Burrows et al. (2004) 7.

24 Nugent (2003) 64.

25 Burrows et al. (2004) 14.

26 European and External Relations Committee, Official Report, 22 March 2005: Col 1210.

> treaty would place an obligation on the UK Government, as a member state, to consult regions with devolved legislative competence, and the UK Government made it clear in evidence to the House of Lords and in the paper that Peter Hain presented that it is content to do so. In answer to a parliamentary question, I said that I had had discussions with the Minister for Europe on the matter, at which he confirmed that the UK Government is keen for devolved Parliaments to have involvement and to develop the mechanisms that would ensure that such involvement worked.[27]

Certainly exploring the extent to which the UK parliament was obligated to consult the Scottish parliament in relation to the protocol on subsidiarity remains a valid source of criticism. As the minister stated several times during his evidence, the UK government has consistently reiterated its desire 'to comply' with the Treaty and develop 'mechanisms that will allow the principle of subsidiarity to be applied'.[28]

The exact details of how the subsidiarity mechanisms would be implemented are the subject of ongoing negotiations between officials from both the UK and Scottish parliaments. However, the initial discussions raise a number of important issues that warrant further consideration. Perhaps the most important issue facing the Scottish parliament is to ensure the protocol operates in such a way that will provide it with ample opportunity to consider the subsidiarity implications of European legislation that relate to devolved matters. Thus, a key issue is whether the six-week timeframe as set out in both the Constitutional Treaty and the UK government's EU bill, is sufficient to ensure that the views of the Scottish parliament are transmitted in a timely and comprehensive manner.

The initial proposals put forward by the House of Commons' European scrutiny committee observe that when considering the subsidiarity implications of European legislation that impinges upon devolved matters, neither the Scottish parliament nor its committees have a 'direct right of appeal'. It is therefore 'essential' that the Scottish parliament 'makes full use' of the rights the Constitutional Treaty has bestowed upon the UK parliament. As the scrutiny committee noted, the UK parliament is obligated 'to respond within 6 weeks', thus any decisions taken out with that timescale will be deemed 'worthless'.[29] Although the subsidiarity protocol has provided the UK parliament with six weeks in which to transmit its opinions on issues relating to subsidiarity, the Scottish parliament is obligated to work within a narrower timeframe. A more realistic timeframe is perhaps between two and three weeks. Thus, as was correctly pointed out by the European scrutiny committee of the Commons, 'if the Scottish Parliament and/or its committees is to input views on a Scottish dimension to the question of subsidiarity, it would have to work extremely quickly'.[30]

---

[27] Ibid.

[28] European and External Relations Committee, Official Report, 22 March 2005: Col 1211.

[29] Scottish Parliament (2003b).

[30] Ibid.

The problem of time is regularly cited as a barrier that hinders effective parliamentary involvement in the scrutiny of European affairs.[31] For example, the issue of timing contributed to the practical problems the Scottish European and external relations committee encountered as it attempted to develop an effective pre-legislative scrutiny procedure. Indeed, a number of similarities exist between the proposals for the implementation of the subsidiarity mechanisms and the challenges the committee faced in undertaking the pre-legislative scrutiny of EC/EU documents.

In 1999, the membership fully expected that the committee's views would be fed directly into the Westminster scrutiny cycle. However, between 1999 and 2003 the committee did not transmit its opinion on a single legislative proposal to the Commons' European scrutiny committee. The recommendation that the committee would implement such a procedure overlooked specific problems associated with the pre-legislative scrutiny of EC/EU documents. The most obvious was that the effectiveness of such a procedure depended upon the Scottish European and external relations committee being able to transmit its views to the UK parliament and government before the matter was discussed in the EU Council of Ministers. Early in the life of the committee's scrutiny procedure it became apparent that 'there was insufficient time' for it to 'transmit opinions to the Commons' committee'.[32]

To ensure the Scottish parliament has the opportunity to consider subsidiarity implications of EU legislation and respond within the restrictive timeframe, effective procedures for the efficient transfer of information still need to be developed. Under the Constitutional Treaty, national parliaments will be entitled to receive a range of papers, documents and information, including Commission consultation documents, the annual legislative programme, instruments of legislative planning or policy, and draft legislative acts. When the UK parliament receives these documents they will be simultaneously sent to the Scottish parliament and its European and external relations committee. To aid the transfer of this information, the Commons' European scrutiny committee proposed two specific mechanisms. The first anticipated that when a member of the House of Commons' staff 'encounter a document to which an objection may be made', the devolved bodies will be alerted 'as early as possible'. The second outlined procedures that would ensure that when 'the devolved bodies identify subsidiarity problems' with a particular piece of legislation, the European scrutiny committee 'will be willing to rescind clearance of the EU legislative proposal and initiate the procedure for objecting on subsidiarity grounds'.[33]

It is equally important that the timely transfer of information also includes the UK government's explanatory memorandum. The memorandum, which acts as the 'trigger' for parliamentary scrutiny, represents a UK minister's evidence

[31] See Carter (2000).

[32] Raunio and Wright (2002), 16.

[33] Scottish Parliament (2003b).

to the UK parliament. Its content will assess the likely impact of a specific proposal and outline the government's policy towards it.[34] The government, through the relevant Whitehall department, is required to submit an explanatory memorandum within ten days of a document being deposited in parliament. In this respect, the European scrutiny committee is almost wholly reliant on the existence of a relationship based upon trust and goodwill between itself and the various Whitehall departments.[35] At present the convention is for an explanatory memorandum to be delivered to the Scottish parliament within ten days. However it is questionable whether a wait of ten days will leave sufficient time for questions of subsidiarity to be adequately considered within a timeframe of between two and three weeks which will be available to the Scottish parliament.

Once the Scottish parliament has received the necessary information, it is equally important that internal procedures are developed that ensure the efficient and effective processing of documents. To this effect, a briefing paper produced by the European and external relations committee[36] outlined three possible procedures, which would enable the parliament to consider subsidiarity issues. The first proposal was for the assessment and final decision to be taken within the committee. The second suggested that the matter could be referred to the Scottish subject committees whose remit the proposed legislation fell under. The third suggested that time be allocated in the chamber for either a short motion or a motion without debate on the issue of whether to object to a particular piece of EU legislation.

The opinion of the Commons' European scrutiny committee was that when working within the six-week timeframe, it was only the Scottish European and external relations committee that would be able to 'systematically undertake an analysis of identifying possible non-compliant proposals'.[37] Given a likely timeframe of between two and three weeks that the Scottish parliament will have to consider these issues, handing sole responsibility to the committee is perhaps the most logical solution. Whether it would be possible, when working within such a restrictive timeframe, to reach a decision via a plenary debate or via presenting a motion without debate remains questionable. There is no evidence of this procedure being used in the Scottish parliament's pre-legislative scrutiny of EU legislation.

Similarly, involving other parliamentary committees in the scrutiny of draft EU legislation presents a number of difficulties. A succinct analysis of these problems was provided to the House of Commons' European scrutiny committee by the then chairman of the trade and industry committee Martin O'Neill. As he noted:

---

34 HC 152 2002, *European Scrutiny in the Commons*, Thirtieth Report for the European Scrutiny Committee Session 2001-2, par. 9.

35 Carter (2000).

36 Scottish Parliament (2004).

37 Scottish Parliament (2003b).

> The difficulties of doing this are not widely understood outside Westminster, comprising basically the problem of synchronising a Committee's timetable to the sometimes capricious legislative timetable of the Council of Ministers and the European Parliament, and the fact that Select Committees greatly prize their power to choose their own programme of activity.[38]

The same procedural difficulties can be applied to Scottish parliamentary committees. Whilst the initial findings regarding the involvement of Scottish parliamentary committees in the scrutiny of EU legislation were considered by the European and external relations committee to be encouraging, it was also noted that there was significant scope for improvement. As the then convenor Irene Oldfather explained, 'as the committees begin more to work together, there are more opportunities for them to do a little bit more scrutiny'.[39]

It is possible to provide an updated assessment of the involvement of other parliamentary committees in the scrutiny of draft EU legislation. At its third meeting in 2002, the European and external relations committee adopted a new scrutiny procedure whereby it no longer recorded a decision or made a recommendation on each document. Instead, a list of all EC/EU documents received by the Scottish parliament and classified by reference to the remits of the Scottish parliamentary committees is published fortnightly. Thereafter, it is for the other parliamentary committees to choose which documents, if any, they wish to examine from the published list. An analysis of this procedure indicates that the increased involvement of other parliamentary committees in the scrutiny of EU legislation has not materialised. The environment and rural development committee and both the justice committees are the only parliamentary committees who routinely overview EU policy developments.

There are a number of lessons to be learned from the Scottish parliament's record in conducting pre-legislative scrutiny that are applicable to the current debate on subsidiarity. Certainly, for the proposed formal mechanisms to operate effectively, the problems that emanate from the six-week timeframe have to be addressed. This proved a difficult barrier to overcome in relation to pre-legislative scrutiny and it can be assumed that similar problems may emerge in relation to subsidiarity. As with pre-legislative scrutiny, the key for effective parliamentary procedures that allow the Scottish parliament to influence subsidiarity decisions is for the parliament to enter the legislative process at the earliest possible stage, and be selective in what issues it chooses to consider. Thus, the parliament may have to adopt a more proactive approach than the proposed formal mechanisms allow. For as Burrows et al. (2004: 26) argue:

> The crucial point regarding subsidiarity and EU governance is that subsidiarity should be regarded as a dynamic – a procedure, a process – for assigning competence between different levels of governance rather than as a rule. Whilst guide-

[38] HC 152 2002, footnote 34 *supra*, Appendix.

[39] European and External Relations Committee, Official Report, 21 May 2002: Col 1554.

lines can be established, in the final instance the political nature of subsidiarity in its application must involve a meaningful dialogue between governments and parliaments at each of the alternative governance levels – supranational, national, and sub-national.

8 Conclusion

This contribution has assessed how and to what extent the Scottish parliament participated in the process to negotiate and ratify the EU Constitutional Treaty. With no formal role it was important that the Scottish parliament utilised alternative mechanisms that ensured its voice was heard throughout this process. Despite past problems in the 'partnership' between the Scottish parliament, the Scottish executive and the UK government, the Scottish parliament and in particular its European and external relations committee appeared satisfied that the views of parliament on regional issues were adequately reflected in both the negotiating position adopted by the UK government and in the final text of the Constitutional Treaty.

To a certain extent 'partnership' was the principal mechanism used to ensure Scottish parliamentary involvement in the Treaty process. However, as this contribution has demonstrated, the Scottish parliament, or more specifically its European and external relations committee, was prepared to move beyond UK channels in order to secure participation. The most prominent examples in this respect were the reports published by the committee. The recommendations contained within these reports were not only aimed at UK channels, but were a concerted attempt to address a wider European audience. Indeed, in collaboration with its counterpart in the Catalan parliament, the Scottish European and external relations committee was able to submit a paper on regional issues, which was debated in the Convention on the future of Europe. Of course there are specific difficulties attached to any attempt to measure extent to which the Scottish parliament was able to influence the final Treaty. However, what this analysis has been able to demonstrate, is the mechanisms by which the Scottish parliament was able to inject its opinions into the Treaty process.

With no separate Scottish bill required to implement the Treaty, Scottish scrutiny of the UK government's EU bill takes on added significance. Issues related to questions on subsidiarity have featured prominently in this scrutiny. The discussion of the procedures that would enable the Scottish dimension on questions of subsidiarity to be considered highlighted a number of important lessons that can be learned from the Scottish parliament's pre-legislative scrutiny of EC/EU documents. In particular, consideration of the problem that time has on the parliamentary scrutiny of EU affairs is relevant. Whilst national parliaments have a timeframe of six weeks in which to operate, the Scottish parliament will have between two and three weeks in which to consider questions of subsidiarity, and to transmit any opinions to Westminster. Thus, for procedures to operate effectively, the Scottish parliament must adopt a proactive approach towards subsidiarity ensuring it enters the legislative process at the earliest opportunity and is selective in what issues it chooses to consider.

References

- N. Burrows, C. Carter and A. Scott, *Subsidiarity and the Draft Treaty*, Report prepared for the Scottish Executive, Sub Rosa, Brussels, 27 April 2004.
- http://www.scotland.gov.uk/about/UNASS/UNASS/00015181/SRSubsid2004.pdf
- C. Carter 'Democratic Governance Beyond the Nation State: Third Level Assemblies and Scrutiny of European Legislation', 6 *European Public Law* (2000) 429-459.
- L. Hooghe and G. Marks, *Multi-Level Governance and European Integration* (Oxford 2001).
- C. Jeffery 'Conclusions: Sub-National Authorities and European Domestic Policy', in C. Jeffery (ed.), *The Regional Dimension of the European Union* (London 1997).
- D. Judge and D. Earnshaw, *The European Parliament* (Basingstoke 2003).
- G. Marks, F. Nielson, L. Ray and J. Salk 'Competencies, Cracks and Conflicts: Regional Mobilization in the European Union', in G. Marks, F. W. Scharpf, P. C. Schmitter and W. Streeck (eds) *Governance in the European Union* (London 1996).
- T. Raunio, T. and A.Wright, *Comparing the EU Committees of Nordic and Scottish Parliaments,* paper presented at the Third Scottish-Nordic Research Network Conference, Aberdeen, 24-25 May 2002.
- B. Rosamond, *Theories of European Integration* (Basingstoke 2000).
- Scottish Executive Press Release SE5065/2001, 15 December 2001.
- Scottish Office, *Handling of European Business* Draft Consultation Paper CSG (98) 74 (1998).
- Scottish Parliament, *Report on the Governance of the European Union and the Future of Europe: What Role for Scotland*, ninth report (2001)
- Scottish Parliament, *The Scottish Parliament and the Convention on the Future of Europe*, Briefing Paper 02/87 (2002a).
- Scottish Parliament, *Scotland's Participation in the Future of Europe Debate – Laeken and the IGC*, Briefing Paper 02/20 (2002b).
- Scottish Parliament, European and External Relations Committee, *Report on the Future of Europe*, sixth report (2002c).
- Scottish Parliament, European and External Relations Committee, *Proposals to Establish a Pan-European network of European Affairs Committees in Regional/Sub-Member State Parliaments*, Briefing Paper EU/02/9/6 (2002d).
- Scottish Parliament, European and External Relations Committee, *Executive's Response to the Committee's 5th Report 2002*, Briefing Paper EU/03/3/1 (2003a).
- Scottish Parliament, European and External Relations Committee, *Convenor's Report*, Briefing Paper EU/S2/03/3/4 Annex A (2003b).
- Scottish Parliament, European and External Relations Committee, *Briefing Paper on Subsidiarity Early Warning*, Briefing Paper EU/S2/O4/1413 (2004).
- Scottish Parliament, *Sewel Motions: Session 1*, Scottish Parliament Fact Sheet FS4-06 (2005).

CHAPTER 4

Parliamentarism, Subsidiarity and Devolution

A Rejoinder

Caitríona A. Carter

The remarks in this rejoinder are aimed at considering two main questions raised by the preceding chapters, Adam Cygan's contribution on the United Kingdom and Gordon Heggie's contribution on Scotland. First, I re-visit the question of the precise type of parliamentary engagement anticipated by the EU Constitutional Treaty protocol on subsidiarity and proportionality in the context of the UK, offering a perspective derived from public policy and political readings of this principle. Second, I suggest areas to which future research programmes might be directed in the absence of a Treaty-defined 'constitutional project' becoming institutionalised across the EU. In so doing, I offer some reflections on the comparative methodologies deployed by the authors for assessing parliamentary engagement in this regard.

Processes of Change and Parliamentary Engagement: Qualifying Subsidiarity as Change

Discussions of UK domestic parliamentary engagement in EU processes must be conducted within a broader context of change in the organisation of the UK polity. Recent developments at EU level unfold against a domestic political environment in which the 'role' for parliaments is in a continuous process of being constituted in response to UK-level reform processes as well as EU-level change – namely, the processes of modernisation, which resulted in a key shift in UK parliamentary approaches to EU scrutiny within Westminster in 1998, and devolution, which established new assemblies in Wales and Northern Ireland, as well as the Scottish parliament. Within this context, the challenge of self-defining as a parliamentary institution in transformation is posed differently from the perspective of Westminster than from the perspective of the Scottish parliament. For as Cygan elucidates, UK parliamentarians within a 'well-established/traditional' national parliament often aim to embed new reforms into existing parliamentary traditions, but do so in a context of modernisation, which brings with it the development of new domestic approaches. This stands by contrast to parliamentary approaches adopted within the relatively 'new' institution of the Scottish parliament as discussed by Heggie, whereby parliamentarians' quest for the definition of their role as a parliament is at the very heart of their response to EU-level reforms.

Against this background, what potential do the new provisions of the EU protocol on subsidiarity and proportionality offer parliaments in terms of their changing engagement in a multi-actor institutional system – what 'parliamentary role' is defined by this protocol? Under the provisions of the protocol, national parliaments are provided with new political opportunities to engage in an improved scrutiny of the European Commission's application of subsidiarity as a legislative tool when proposing legislation. No formal standing is accorded regional parliaments in this regard – rather national parliaments *may* consult regional parliaments with legislative powers. To clarify subsidiarity in this context, Article I-11 of the Constitutional Treaty distinguishes between the principle of conferral, on the one hand, and the principle of subsidiarity, on the other: 'The *limits* of Union competences are governed by the principle of conferral. The *use* of Union competences is governed by the principles of subsidiarity and proportionality' (emphasis added).[1]

Subsidiarity is further defined as follows:

> '[I]n areas which do not fall within its exclusive competence, the Union shall act only if and insofar as the objectives of the proposed action cannot be sufficiently achieved by the Member States, either at central level or at regional and local level, but can rather, by reason of the scale or effects of the proposed action, be better achieved at Union level'.[2]

Scrutiny of the application of subsidiarity thus brings national parliaments, and regional parliaments, into a political dialogue with the Commission, and with each other, over the specific question whether 'the objectives of the intended action can be *better achieved* at Union level'? More precisely, a meaningful political application of subsidiarity in this context would require Community institutions and national and regional parliaments to be engaged in an on-going dialogue on the exercise of shared competences, and with the aim of that dialogue to generate *consensus* over the decision taken.[3]

An interpretation of this application of subsidiarity from a public policy and political perspective would envisage such a dialogue being premised on three core questions:[4] First, 'what criteria should be used to defend a decision to legislate at EU level?'; second, 'what is the best type of legal instrument to be used?';[5] third, 'which actors should be involved in the taking of these two decisions?'. From this reading, subsidiarity emerges as a 'device for managing competing claims for the assignment of competences between different tiers in a multi-level system',[6] when that competence is deemed shared. Accordingly, different scenarios can be envisaged whereby parliaments might mount

1 According to Piris, member of the European Convention working group on subsidiarity, '[T]his principle is intended to regulate the exercise of competence and not state whether competence exists in a particular area' and 'is an essentially political and subjective principle', CONV WG I, WD 04, 3 July 2002, p. 8.

2 Article I-11 (2) of the Constitutional Treaty.

3 See Burrows et al. (2004) 26.

4 See Burrows et al. (2004) 7.

5 This is correctly the test of proportionality, but see Burrows et al. (2004) 12, where attention is drawn to the ruling in Case C-491/01 *R* v *Secretary of State for Health ex parte BAT*, where the ECJ held that the question of the 'intensity of action' comes under the scope of subsidiarity. See also the contribution by Adam Cygan in this volume.

6 See Burrows et al. (2004) 7.

a challenge to a Commission proposal on grounds of subsidiarity:[7] for example, parliaments might challenge the Commission's justification for common action as set out in its impact assessment within its explanatory memorandum with regard to the costs of proposed legislation, or a poverty of analysis of local impact; a challenge might be raised on the grounds of the costs of the proposed legislation, when the costs are considered to fall disproportionately to a state or region given the nature of its economic base; a challenge might be raised when a parliament considers that there has been a consistent level of policy failure at EU level, and that a de-centralised, i.e. national or regional regulatory solution be preferred; or, a challenge might be mounted on the type of legal instrument proposed. Engaging in this way would require a particular type of parliamentary adaptation to bring subsidiarity into parliamentary 'consciousness'.[8] This would entail *inter alia* the consideration of whether the parliamentary function in this instance would be to scrutinise its own government's position on the above considerations, or whether a parliamentary committee would wish to put resources towards directly engaging in impact assessment discussions, including the conduct of reviews of the costs of legislation. Reflecting upon the 'goal' of *ex ante* parliamentary EU scrutiny already operating within a parliament might therefore form a critical part of that process.

Finally, any modalities developed between parliaments to enable dialogue to be constructed might themselves have effects on the process of self-definition of parliaments in situations of change. In particular, engaging in inter-parliamentary procedures – whether at EU level or internally within the UK – might orientate parliamentarians and European affairs committees towards self-defining as 'parliaments within a multi-level institutional order of parliaments' – a process which could itself result in internal change for the handling of EU affairs.[9]

Future Research Agendas: Methodologies for Assessing Parliamentary Engagement

Assessing the impact of EU-level reforms, such as the ones discussed above, requires some further reflection upon the appropriateness of existing frameworks for analysis. Considering the two contributions by Cygan and Heggie, we see that they are each located within distinct scholarly contexts and adopt very different approaches to assessing change in parliamentary engagement. National parliamentary adaptation to the EU is the field of enquiry of an extensive literature in which the nature and effects of change at the national level are the subject of intense scholarly debate.[10] Within these debates,

7 The following is drawn from Burrows et al. (2004) 21.

8 See Burrows et al. (2004) 34 (plenary discussions).

9 This is the experience for the assembly in Wales, see, for example, Carter (2005).

10 See, for example, Maurer and Wessels (2001); Kerse (2000); Norton (1996); Judge (1995).

the approach adopted by Cygan is a formalistic one – to provide a comprehensive and representational legalistic overview of past UK parliamentary engagement, and define parliamentary adaptation in terms of the development of new formal mechanisms and rules of engagement. This approach stands alongside (new) institutionalist-based accounts of parliamentary change which dominate the literature, but where the focus of empirical research is rather on the very question of the effectiveness of 'rules in practice' – for example, the extent to which the British scrutiny reserve acts as an effective mechanism of accountability – or where informal definitions of institutions, such as unwritten rules, shared values or cognitive scripts, are considered important variables in assessments of change.[11] Within this analytical debate, a clearer specification of the 'added value' of the 'formalistic approach' and its positioning *vis-á-vis* other frameworks would be welcomed. What 'issues' or 'empirical puzzles' does this approach identify which other more 'institutionalist' approaches do not?

By contrast to the work on national parliamentary adaptation to EU processes, little research has been conducted on regional parliaments, although there is a growing body of work on the role of both the Scottish parliament and the national assembly for Wales in this regard.[12] Frameworks developed specifically for the assessment of national parliaments have their limitations when applied to assessments of regional parliaments in EU processes.[13] The approach adopted by Heggie is informative in this regard. Drawing from both the literature on multi-level governance in general, and institutionalist accounts on regional parliamentary engagement in particular, the approach is to consider adaptation via the application of the conceptual tool of 'partnership' and the institutionalist variable of 'time'. Within this approach, greater attention might be accorded to other variables which define future parliamentary engagement over subsidiarity questions. For example, as is implied above, a parliamentary challenge to a 'best level' decision might require significant resources, organisational capacity, working procedures and understandings for access to information from the Scottish executive, a changed institutional culture to bring 'subsidiarity' into consciousness, e.g. through training, access to data and so on. In short, greater specificity is required here in the consideration of 'other factors' which might affect a regional parliament's ability to engage, and which might be distinct from a national parliament.

Overall, a clearer connotation of research frameworks is essential – not only in our own work, but in general in the assessment of changing parliamentary engagement in EU affairs. Greater specificity would be especially fruitful to the generation of inter-disciplinary frameworks located within the disciplines of law and social science for the purposes of generating new research programmes.

---

11 See Carter (2005).

12 See, for example, Carter and McLeod (2005); Carter (2005); Heggie (2003); Randall and Seawright (2002).

13 See Carter and McLeod (2005) 69.

These reflections on frameworks finally encourage one to focus attention on at least two areas for future research. Whilst much of the current debate on national parliaments is caught up in evaluations of high-level constitutional reforms, little attention has been paid to other ongoing processes of change which concern the improvement of the implementation of subsidiarity decisions within the policy cycle. In particular, the EU's 'better regulation strategy'[14] has already resulted in important adjustments being adopted by the Commission – including the development of new policy instruments, such as the tool of the 'integrated impact assessment', and the drive towards improved procedures for external consultation in the pre-legislative phase of the policy process, and in which parliaments could engage over subsidiarity questions. External consultation aims to enhance policy inception, including the exchange of 'ideas', 'and, if conducted as part of the Commission's new impact assessment system, addresses questions of both policy design, future policy (regulatory) options, including the application of subsidiarity considerations'.[15] Engaging in policy inception processes and within the impact assessment system would thus bring parliamentary committees into the dialogue of subsidiarity.[16] Whether and how parliamentary committees are engaging in these pre-legislative systematised processes would be a fruitful area for research. For example, are committees developing thinking on how best to monitor government input to impact assessment, where many subsidiarity-type considerations are resolved prior to the Commission deciding to go down the legislative route?

This leads us on to a second possible area for research, namely whether we can locate an underlying collective 'parliamentary project', which is part of an ongoing parliamentary strategy to improve access to the subsidiarity dialogue, and to which the protocol attached to the Constitutional Treaty is the most visible part? Do domestic parliaments frame institutional adaptations in terms of an ideology of EU polity-building, in which the political dialogue of subsidiarity is an integral part, and which could be identified by researching other avenues of engagement being pursued in the absence of treaty reform? Can we talk about the 'level of commitment of parliamentary committees' to engage in such a 'parliamentary project' irrespective of whether or not the Constitutional Treaty is enforced? These two areas of research thus re-orientate focus towards informal and regulatory processes of 'constitution-building' and ultimately lead us to question the existence or not of a 'parliamentary politics' of subsidiarity.

---

14 Burrows et al (2004b).

15 Ibid., p. 8.

16 Developments of this nature have already taken place in the UK; for example, both the Scottish parliament's and the national assembly for Wales' European committees use the Commission's work programme to guide scrutiny choices; the Welsh European committee has also engaged in the impact assessment process as part of its scrutiny process, e.g. on the working time directive.

References

- N. Burrows, C. Carter and A. Scott, *Subsidiarity and the Draft Treaty*, Report prepared for the Scottish Executive, Sub Rosa, Brussels, 27 April 2004.
- http://www.scotland.gov.uk/about/UNASS/UNASS/00015181/SRSubsid2004.pdf
- N. Burrows, C. Carter, M. Fletcher and A. Scott (2004b), *The Better Regulation Strategy*, Report prepared for the Scottish Executive, Sub Rosa, Brussels, 22 October 2004.
- C. Carter, *Identifying Causality in Institutional Change: the Adaptation of the National Assembly for Wales to the European Union*, paper presented at CRAPE/IEP de Rennes, 8 December 2005.
- C. Carter and A. McLeod, 'The Scottish Parliament and the European Union: Analysing Regional Parliamentary Engagement' in S. Weatherill and U. Bernitz (eds), *The Role of the Regions and Sub-National Actors in Europe* (Oxford 2005).
- G. Heggie, 'The story so far: the role of the Scottish Parliament's European Committee in the UK-EU policy cycle', 44 *Scottish Affairs* (2003), pp. 114-131.
- D. Judge, 'The Failure of National Parliaments?' in J. Hayward (ed.), *The Crisis of Representation of Europe* (London 1995).
- C.S. Kerse, 'Parliamentary Scrutiny of the Third Pillar' 6 *European Public Law* (2000), pp. 81-101.
- Ph. Norton, 'The UK: Political Conflict, Parliamentary Scrutiny' in Ph. Norton (ed.), *National Parliaments and the EU* (London 1996).
- A. Maurer and W. Wessels (eds), *National Parliaments on their Ways to Europe: Losers or Latecomers?*, (Baden-Baden 2001).
- N. Randall and D. Seawright, *Merely a talking shop? The European Committees of the Scottish Parliament and Welsh Assembly: 'New Politics' in a system of multi-level governance?*, paper presented at the Annual Conference of the Political Studies Association, University of Aberdeen, 5-7 April 2002.

CHAPTER 5

The Belgian 'National Parliament' from the Perspective of the EU Constitutional Treaty

Wouter Pas

1 Introduction

'Belgium wishes to make clear that, in accordance with its constitutional law, not only the Chamber of Representatives and Senate of the Federal Parliament but also the parliamentary assemblies of the Communities and the Regions act, in terms of the competences exercised by the Union, as components of the national parliamentary system or chambers of the national Parliament.'

This declaration by the Kingdom of Belgium on national parliaments, annexed to the final act of the Treaty establishing a Constitution for Europe, poses clearly the particular problems of the involvement of the Belgian parliaments in the process of adopting the Treaty, and in the implementation of specific procedures within the European treaties. The declaration states that all the parliamentary assemblies act as components of the national parliamentary system or as chambers of the national parliament. In order to understand this, it is necessary to give a short introduction to the Belgian constitutional system, and to the role that its component units and its parliaments are to play at the international and European level (section 2). Afterwards, in section 3, we will examine some effects of Belgian federalism on the adoption and possible implementation of the Constitutional Treaty. There the role of the 'national parliament(s)' in the Convention, in the ratification process, and in the information and consultation procedures will be explored.

2 Belgian Federalism

Belgian federalism is based on exclusive powers granted to either federal or sub-national authorities. This paradigm leads to an allocation of corresponding external powers on the basis of the notion *'in foro interno, in foro externo'*. This principle also applies to the involvement of parliaments in external policy.

2.1 Federalism based on Strictly Exclusive Powers

The Belgian federal structure[1] is based on a centrifugal or devolutionary federalism, grown out of the bipolar division of the country in a French-speaking and a Dutch-speaking population. This bipolar division not only transformed a unitary state into a federal state by creating sub-national entities. It also led to a federal authority that is organised in a confederal way, by equalising the French-speaking minority to the Dutch-speaking majority via an elaborate system of parity, special majorities and blocking procedures. The rules

[1] On Belgian federalism see e.g. Alen (1993); Alen and Ergec (1998); Delmartino (1996); Deschouwer (2005); Goudappel (1998); Pas (2004); Peeters (1994).

of this federal system are laid down in the Belgian constitution[2] and in various so-called special majority acts.[3] The most important of these special majority acts is that of 8 August 1980 'reforming the institutions',[4] hereinafter referred to as the special institutional reform act.

The Belgian federal structure is dual-layered. It features two types of sub-national entities: three regions and three communities. The Flemish, Walloon and Brussels-Capital regions, on the one hand, and the Flemish, French and German-speaking communities, on the other hand, have a distinct, sometimes overlapping territory, but in both cases the three of them together cover the whole Belgian territory. Within the bilingual region of Brussels the powers of the communities are distributed and exercised in a complicated way. Both the French and the Flemish community have important powers, but only with regard to institutions or organisations. With regard to individual persons, or bilingual institutions and organisations, the powers are attributed to the federal authority or the joint community commission. In some fields the French community has passed the exercise of its powers in Brussels-Capital to the French community commission.[5]

Communities and regions are vested with different powers,[6] which are in principle strictly separated.[7] As noted, the powers of the communities and the regions are attributed by the constitution and the special majority acts. Residuary power belongs to the federal authority.[8] As due in a federal system, the communities and regions have their own institutions and their own powers, which are not subordinated to the federal institutions and powers. The sub-national institutions, parliaments and governments, are vested with legislative and executive powers. The legislative power, executed by parliament and government together, through so-called decrees,[9] is equal to that of the federal legis-

---

2 The main amendments took place in 1970, 1980, 1988 and 1993.

3 According to Article 4 of the constitution, a special majority act requires, besides an overall two-thirds majority in each house of the federal parliament, a majority in each language group within the House of Representatives and the Senate.

4 This act underwent important changes, especially in 1988, 1993 and 2001.

5 The French community commission (COCOF) and the Flemish community commission are in origin administrative, executive bodies, subordinated to their respective communities.

6 The communities have powers in matters like education, language legislation, cultural, health, family and social policy (see Articles 127-130 of the constitution and Article 4-5 of the special institutional reform act). The regions have powers with regard to economic and employment policy, environmental and energy policy, agricultural policy, local authorities, roads, transport, etc. (see especially Article 6 of the special institutional reform act).

7 Article 39 of the Belgian constitution.

8 Article 35 of the constitution transfers the residual powers to the communities and/or regions, but this Article has not yet entered into force.

9 The acts of parliament of the Brussels-Capital region and of the assembly of the joint community commission in Brussels-Capital are called 'ordinances'. They have a slightly weaker legal force.

lature. Sub-national decrees have the same legal authority as a federal statute within their field of competence. This legal equality of federal, community and regional laws is a distinguishing characteristic of the Belgian federal system. It does not know a principle of federal supremacy like the German *'Bundesrecht bricht Landesrecht'* principle. The absence of federal supremacy goes hand in hand with the general rule of exclusiveness in the division of powers, and a very limited use of concurrent powers. The principle of exclusivity means that there is a strict separation between the powers of the federal state, the regions and the communities. *Ratione materiae* as well as *ratione loci*, for a given matter one and only one authority can have jurisdiction. Each power has been assigned to one entity only. If certain matters relate to several competences, the qualification applied will be that of the concept of competences with which the provision is most strongly related.[10]

Given this strict separation of powers, and the strict legal equality of federal and sub-national law, an elaborate system of co-operation is necessary. The special institutional reform act introduced many optional and mandatory forms of co-operation. The most important form consists of optional and mandatory co-operation agreements. These co-operation agreements cannot alter the system of distribution of exclusive powers, but are meant to regulate and structure the exercise of powers of the various levels. The various levels can decide to jointly exercise their powers, or commit themselves to exercise them in a certain manner. Both the principle of exclusive distribution of powers, as that of close (and often mandatory) co-operation, play a crucial role with regard to the external powers of communities and regions.

2.2 External Powers based on the Idea of *'in foro interno, in foro externo'*

The starting point in the allocation of external powers to Belgian state entities is the parallel between the allocation of powers at the internal, national level, and the powers at the international level. The aim of giving and protecting the autonomy of the sub-national entities has been achieved by a very strict parallelism in the distribution of powers at the domestic and the international level, according to the so-called *'in foro interno, in foro externo'* principle. This principle is only set aside for some very limited powers of the federal government to co-ordinate Belgian foreign policy. This principle, and its application, which lead to exceptionally far-reaching powers in the field of external relations for the regions and the communities, is completed with techniques of co-operative federalism.[11]

The Belgian constitution states that the King, i.e. the federal government, manages international relations. However, the constitution adds that this power

---

10 Alen and Peeters (1997) 170.

11 Wouters and De Smet (2001) 129.

is 'without prejudice to the ability of Communities and Regions to engage in international co-operation, including the signature of treaties, for those matters within their responsibilities as established by the Constitution and in virtue thereof'.[12] The constitution further specifies that the King concludes treaties, but not those that can or have to be concluded by the communities and regional governments. Sub-national governments conclude, in matters that concern them, treaties regarding matters that are in the scope of the responsibilities of their councils.[13] Following radically the *'in foro interno, in foro externo'* idea, the idea of exclusivity in the internal distribution of powers leads not only to the allocation of powers with the communities and the regions, but also to a prohibition for the Belgian federal government to conclude treaties relating to matters falling within the exclusive powers of the sub-national entities.[14] Many authors consider that 'no other constitution in the world is as progressive and radical to this point'.[15]

However, co-operation plays a crucial role in the whole system. This has a double reason. Many forms of international co-operation and many international treaties deal with matters that belong to different competences across the various levels within the Belgian state, and international organisations in principle will want to deal with the federal state only. Because of the reluctance of other states or international organisations to deal with sub-national entities, Belgian constitutional law created procedures in which the federal authority renders assistance to the sub-national entities in order to act at the international level. This is the case with regard to treaty-making power, especially the making of so-called mixed treaties,[16] and with regard to sub-national representation in international institutions, especially in the European Union.

2.3 Involvement of the Parliaments in External Policy

As is well known, external policy is the playground of the executive powers. Within the Belgian federal system this means that the central role is played by the federal government, and the governments of the regions and communities. However, parliaments have a constitutionally guaranteed right of participation in treaty-making processes.

Article 167 of the Belgian constitution accords treaty-making power to the government of the federal state, as well as to those of the regions and communities. Along with this treaty-making power, the constitution establishes the power of the parliaments to approve or to disapprove treaties concluded by their respective government. An international treaty can only have an internal legal

[12] Article 167 (1) of the constitution.

[13] Article 167 (2) and (3) of the constitution.

[14] The joint community commission in Brussels-Capital constitutes an exception.

[15] Wouters and De Smet (2001) 130; Louis and Alen (1994) 107.

[16] These are treaties concerning both federal matters and matters of the communities and/or regions, or treaties concerning both regional and community matters.

effect if it obtained parliamentary consent.[17] For mixed treaties, this implies approval by all parliaments concerned. For the federal level, a statute approved by both chambers of the federal parliament, the House of Representatives and the Senate, is required.[18] As for the sub-national level, in some cases, like for example the treaties regarding the European Union, the approval of seven sub-national parliaments or assemblies is necessary.[19] Once all the parliaments involved have given their consent, the ratification of the treaty can take place.[20]

Parliamentary consent to treaties is given by a federal statute or by a decree or ordinance of the various parliaments. The drafts of these acts are subject to a mandatory advisory opinion of the Council of State. They are also subject to the control of the constitutional court, the Court of Arbitration. Within the short delay of sixty days, an appeal can be brought before the constitutional court to annul a federal act, a decree or an ordinance approving a treaty. The court also has jurisdiction to examine the respect of the allocation of powers within the framework of a preliminary rulings procedure. The latter implies that even years after ratification of the treaty, the court could consider an approval act unconstitutional. This would imply that a treaty is no longer to apply at the domestic level, whereas it remains in force at the international level. In order to avoid this awkward situation in at least some important cases, the special majority act on the Court of Arbitration excludes the possibility of preliminary rulings with regard to a constituent treaty of the European Union, or with regard to the European Convention on Human Rights and its protocols.[21]

3 The Treaty establishing a Constitution for Europe

3.1 The Constitutional Convention

The nomination of representatives

The Convention on the future of Europe, convened by the European Council in the 2001 declaration of Laken (Laeken), was composed, among

---

17 This rule also goes for the so-called 'executive agreements'. In practice, however, these executive agreements are not always submitted for parliamentary approval.

18 See Article 77 (6) of the constitution.

19 The Flemish parliament (i.e. the merged assembly for both the Flemish region and community), the Walloon parliament, the parliament of the French community, the parliament of the Brussels-Capital region, the parliament of the German-speaking community, the assembly of the French community commission in the Brussels-Capital region, and the assembly of the Brussels-Capital joint community commission.

20 According to the co-operation agreement of 8 March 1994, the federal minister of foreign affairs will draw up Belgium's instrument of ratification, and submit it to the King for ratification.

21 Article 26 (1) *bis* of the special majority act on the Court of Arbitration.

others, of thirty members of the national parliaments. Two of the full members of the Belgian delegation[22] were the representatives of the Belgian federal parliament. Although it was not explicitly stated in the Laken declaration, this national parliamentary representation was understood as calling for one representative of the House and one of the Senate.

The way the representatives of the Belgian parliaments were nominated is quite illustrative for the position of parliaments within the European constitutional process. In fact, the federal government, without consulting the parliament, appointed the chairmen of the largest Flemish and francophone political parties. These chairmen did not hold a seat in the federal parliament. One of them held a seat in the Flemish regional parliament, the other one had no parliamentary mandate whatsoever. This decision led to critical reactions, so that eventually it was left to the parliament to appoint its representatives. As a result, the parliament nominated these same two party chairmen as its representatives. The House of Representatives only expressed its discontent by not accepting one of the substitutes proposed by the government.

The fact that the parliamentary representatives were not members of the federal parliament led to a parliamentary discussion on the question whether or not is was compatible with the declaration of Laken to consider a regional MP as a 'member of national parliament' in the sense of this declaration. In the parliamentary discussions reference was made to a legal advice given by distinguished legal scholar and ECJ judge Koen Lenaerts to the federal prime minister. According to this advice, the declaration, being a decision of the European Council, cannot interfere with the internal constitutional order of member states. Every member state should determine itself what directly elected parliamentary assemblies should be considered components of what is called by the declaration a 'national parliament'. It is legitimate for the House of Representatives to state that within the specific Belgian constitutional order the parliaments of the regions and communities are not subordinate to the House or the Senate, but that they are, within their jurisdiction, coordinate. It is up to the House[23] to decide whether a member of the Flemish parliament can be considered a member of the national parliament.[24]

The position of the representatives

The Belgian delegation, to which the two representatives of the federal parliament and their two substitutes belonged, was strongly co-ordinated by the federal ministry of foreign affairs.[25] Due to this co-ordination, the Belgian

[22] Belgium had eleven members in the Convention: five with full membership, three substitutes, and three members with the status of observer.

[23] It is not clear on what ground the House is entitled to decide solely about this representation, given the mentioned coordinate character of international powers.

[24] Advice quoted in Parliamentary Proceedings (*Handelingen*), Senate, 2-182, 21 February 2002.

[25] Bursens (2005) 70-74.

conventioneers defended for the most part common, or at least congruent, positions. According to Delreux, this was due *inter alia* to the fact that the chambers of the Belgian federal parliament did not provide a mandate to their representatives. They neither installed a monitoring body nor a forum where the Convention members had to defend their actions and positions in the Convention.[26] The absence of control mechanisms left space for the central role of the federal ministry of foreign affairs. All this leads to the conclusion that, as far as Belgium is concerned, there was no feedback and no real parliamentary representation in the Convention. The conclusion seems to confirm the general assessment that there is a low degree of attention given by the parliamentary bodies to European policy, and that in a comparative perspective on the role of national parliaments in European policy-making, Belgian parliaments, both federal and sub-national, are to be classified as being weak.[27]

3.2 The Ratification Process

'Mixed' treaty

European treaties, and *a fortiori* the Constitutional Treaty, are 'mixed treaties' since they deal with both federal and sub-national matters. The Constitutional Treaty, according to the constitutional rules mentioned earlier, has to be approved by nine legislative bodies. No ratification by Belgium is possible if the approval of one of these bodies is missing. The Constitutional Treaty has in fact already received all required approvals, namely from the Senate (28 April 2005), the House of Representatives (19 May 2005), by ordinance from the parliament of the Brussels-Capital region (23 June 2005), by ordinance from the joint assembly of the joint community commission (23 June 2005), by decree from the parliament of the German-speaking community (20 June 2005), by two decrees[28] of the parliament of the Walloon region (30 June 2005), by decree from the parliament of the French language community (20 July 2005), by decree from the French community commission (20 July 2005) and by decree from the Flemish parliament (8 February 2006).

The parliamentary debates on the approval of the Constitutional Treaty were coloured, not to say overshadowed, by two internal constitutional debates: one on the need for, or the possibility of, a referendum (see below), and one on the co-operation agreement with regard to the role of the national parliaments in the information and consultation mechanisms provided for by the Constitutional Treaty. In fact, the delayed consent of the Flemish parliament was due to the fact that the Flemish government, and the parliamentary majority that supports it, were of the opinion that the conclusion of a co-operation agreement with regard

26 Delreux (2005) 12.

27 Bursens (2002) 577.

28 One concerning regional matters, one concerning community matters transferred by the French community.

to the role of the national parliaments, including the Flemish parliament, was a preliminary condition for the Flemish approval of the Constitutional Treaty.[29] This agreement, which we will discuss in detail in section 4.3, was signed by the chairmen of eight involved assemblies on 19 December 2005, and it was approved by the Flemish parliament three days later.[30]

Referendum

In both the federal and the Flemish parliament, the issue of a possible referendum on the Constitutional Treaty was debated. In this context, it should be mentioned that according to the traditional doctrine and jurisprudence, a binding referendum is at odds with the Belgian constitution. This opinion was confirmed in an advisory opinion of the section for legislation of the Council of State on a proposed bill concerning a referendum about the Constitutional Treaty.[31] A binding referendum is deemed in contradiction with the system of representative democracy, as implied by Article 33 of the Belgian constitution.[32] Within their constitutional powers, in particular those of Articles 167 (2) and (3), the parliaments cannot be bound by a mandate, not even by a mandate from the people. The constitution in its current form therefore excludes any form of direct democracy. The same goes, according to the Council of State, for consultative referenda. Even if the outcome of a referendum would legally only have the value of an advice to the parliamentary organ, by its importance and its weight the outcome of the referendum would create such a political pressure that it would alter the way in which parliament can execute its constitutional power. This interpretation excludes referenda, both at the federal and the sub-national level. The construction to put – from a legal point of view – a binding referendum on a par with a non-binding referendum is however highly controversial. It is asserted that it is up to the legislator itself to decide what kinds of advice and consultation mechanisms it will install, and how it will take into account these advices. Until today only one consultative referendum took place in Belgian history. According to many politicians and scholars this popular consultation, on the question whether King Leopold III should return to the throne after World War II, was 'traumatic'. As a matter of fact, the referendum showed a profound difference in opinion between the north and the south of the country. The issue of a referendum is therefore, like any other political issue of importance, linked to the diverging opinions in the different parts of Belgium, and to the question how these differences should be taken into account.

---

29 See e.g. policy paper of the Flemish minister of foreign affairs, Parliamentary Documents (Parl.Doc.), Flemish Parliament, 2005-2006, 546/1, 6-7 or Parl. Doc., Flemish Parliament, 2004-2005, 358/3, 6-7.

30 Parl. Doc., Flemish Parliament, 2005-06, 628/1.

31 Advice 37.804/AV of 23 November 2004, Parl. Doc., House of Representatives, 2004-2005, 51-281/4.

32 Article 33 states that 'all power emanates from the Nation and is exerted in the manner established by the Constitution'.

The debate about a referendum was partly based on the merits and disadvantages of a referendum, but also on issues of political balance between coalition partners in the federal government. This led to a rather confusing process in parliament. The political partners in the federal government were divided on the issue of a referendum. The liberal prime-minister was in favour, while the Socialist parties feared the 'oversimplification' that a referendum would imply. Therefore the government did not take a common position, and let the matter to the parliament to decide. At the end of 2004 a majority in the House of Representatives seemed willing to pass an ordinary bill on a consultative referendum, by-passing the opinion of the Council of State. At the end of January 2005 the small Flemish social-liberal coalition partner decided suddenly to drop its previous support for a referendum. The party defended its move by saying that the referendum on the Constitutional Treaty would be abused by the extreme-right, which would seek to transform it into a referendum on Turkish membership of the EU. The parliamentary committee competent for constitutional questions eventually rejected the proposed bill on 16 February 2005.[33] Simultaneously, an amendment of the Belgian constitution was proposed in order to introduce the possibility of consulting the people in the procedure of approving an international treaty;[34][35] this constitutional amendment obtained a relative majority in the plenary session of the House on 10 March 2005,[36] but fell short of the necessary two-thirds majority.

The Flemish parliament also examined proposals on the organisation of a popular consultation within the Flemish community. These proposals were not supported by the Flemish government. The government considered them not opportune, and probably unconstitutional. The proposals were rejected on 21 November 2005.[37]

4 Information and Consultation Mechanisms

4.1 Existing Internal Procedures

In addition to the procedures provided at European level by the Amsterdam protocol on the role of national parliaments in the European Union,

33 Report of the commission for the revision of the constitution and the reform of the institutions, Parl. Doc., House of Representatives, 2004-05,51-281/5, 5 and 48.

34 Parl. Doc., House of Representatives, 2004-2005, 51-1531/1.

35 The amendment did not enable a consultation in general, but only in the specific context of treaties transferring sovereignty. This has to do with the fact that the relevant Article 167 was, according to the Belgian constitutional amendment procedure, open to revision, whereas other Articles, necessary for a general consultation, were not amendable.

36 73 'yes' to 62 'no'.

37 9 to 5 vote, in the parliamentary committee on internal affairs, see Parl. Doc., Flemish Parliament, 2004-2005, 215/3.

some specific internal Belgian procedures of parliamentary involvement can be mentioned. In order to determine the Belgian position in the EU Council of Ministers, all parliaments have the right to be informed by their respective government of every draft or proposal of a legal act of the European Commission or the Council, such as draft regulations and directives. Subsequently the parliaments have the right to give advice to their governments concerning these drafts and proposals.[38] In the specific context of negotiations about a revision of the treaties establishing the European Communities and of the treaties and acts by which these treaties have been amended, all parliaments must be informed right from the start, and they must receive the draft treaties before signature.[39] These information and advice procedures however do not seem to work effectively, although some regional parliaments, especially the Flemish parliament, work actively on the 'subsidiarity monitoring network' set up by the Committee of the Regions in collaboration with the working group on subsidiarity of the conference of regional legislative assemblies of the European Union (CALRE).

4.2 The Constitutional Treaty: Simplified Revision Procedure and Early Warning System on Subsidiarity and Proportionality

Description of the procedures

The so-called 'simplified revision procedure' as included in the Constitutional Treaty gives national parliaments a blocking power. In this procedure the European Council can, by unanimity, and with the consent of the European Parliament, change the EU legislative procedure for a given area, and move from unanimity to qualified majority voting, or move to co-decision with the European Parliament in an area where this does not yet apply. Any initiative taken by the European Council on this basis is to be notified to the national parliaments. If a national parliament makes known its opposition within six months, the decision of the European Council shall not be adopted, according to Article IV-444 of the Constitutional Treaty.[40]

In the context of subsidiarity, national parliaments will, according to the Treaty, have to ensure that certain proposals and legislative initiatives comply with the principle of subsidiarity.[41] They will have to do so in accordance with

---

38 Article 92 *quater* of the special institutional reform act.

39 Article 168 of the constitution and Article 16 (2) of the special institutional reform act.

40 In its explanatory note to the draft act of approval of the Constitutional Treaty, the federal government states that it regrets that these general 'passerelle clauses' are conditioned by the possibility of each national parliament to oppose to it, Parl. Doc., Senate, 2004-2005, 3-1091/1, 109.

41 Under the principle of subsidiarity, in areas which do not fall within its exclusive competence, the Union shall act only if and insofar as the objectives of the proposed action cannot be sufficiently achieved by the member states, either at central level or at regional and local level, but can rather, by reason of the scale or effects of the proposed action, be better achieved at Union level (Article I-11 of the Constitutional Treaty).

the rules laid down in a protocol on the application of the principles of subsidiarity and proportionality.[42] According to Article 6 of this protocol, any national parliament or any chamber of a national parliament may issue a reasoned opinion stating why it considers that a particular draft of a European legislative act does not comply with the principle of subsidiarity.[43] Article 6 adds that it will be for each national parliament or each chamber of a national parliament to consult, where appropriate, regional parliaments with legislative powers. According to Article 7 of the protocol, when incoming reasoned opinions represent at least one third of all the votes allocated to the national parliaments, the draft must be reviewed. The votes are allocated by giving two votes to each national parliament, shared out on the basis of the respective national parliamentary system. In the case of a bicameral parliamentary system, each of the two chambers shall have one vote. Article 8 of the protocol adds that the European Court of Justice has jurisdiction in actions on grounds of infringement of the principle of subsidiarity brought by member states or notified by them in accordance with their legal order on behalf of their national parliament or a chamber of it.

Declaration no. 49

If the above Articles of the Constitutional Treaty on 'national parliaments' are in Belgian context to be read as referring to the federal parliament, and if it were the federal parliament that should, where appropriate, consult the regional and community parliaments, then the resulting procedures would be at odds with the Belgian constitutional order.[44] As mentioned before, in some fields of competences, the Belgian federal parliament has no power at all, neither internally nor externally. Giving a say to the federal parliament in these matters, even during the examination of a European proposal, would imply a violation of the internal allocation of powers. Reducing the involvement of regional parliaments to the right to be consulted is also incompatible with the Belgian constitution, since in such cases the regional parliaments have the exclusive right to decide.

This is why Belgium issued a declaration with respect to 'national parliaments' in the context of the Constitutional Treaty. According to this declaration, labelled final act declaration no. 49, which is quoted at the beginning of this contribution, not only the two chambers of the Belgian federal parliament, but also the parliamentary assemblies of the communities and the regions can act as components of the national parliamentary system or chambers of the national parliament. On the significance of this declaration no. 49, two positions have

---

42 See also Article I-18, III-259 of the Constitutional Treaty.

43 See also Article 3 of the first protocol on the role of national parliaments in the EU.

44 The declaration of Catalonia of 25 October 2005 by the presidents of the regional legislative assemblies of the European Union (CALRE), says: 'In Belgium the state and regional parliaments have the same rights with respect to the subsidiarity principle. Consequently, the procedure proposed in this declaration (i.e. a consulting and conciliation procedure) is a minimum for the Belgian regional parliaments'.

been defended: one by the Belgian Council of State, and one by, *inter alia*, the Belgian federal government.

In its advisory opinion on the legislative acts granting approval to the Constitutional Treaty,[45] the *Council of State* was of the opinion that this declaration is not binding upon the European institutions or other member states of the EU. The Council of State pointed to the fact that the declaration was only noted by the intergovernmental conference and annexed to the final act, whereas other declarations were adopted by the conference. The Council of State also argued that where the Treaty wants to mention parliamentary institutions other than federal or national ones, it explicitly does so. This is the case in the context of the subsidiarity protocol, which refers to regional parliaments with legislative powers.[46] According to the Council of State, the notion of 'parliamentary system' used in the protocols is based upon the assumption of an existing unicameral or bicameral system,[47] which are by definition national or federal. Particularly Article 7 (2) of the subsidiarity protocol works on the hypothesis that a national parliament is composed of a maximum of two chambers. For the Council of State it is uncertain whether the European institutions, as far as Belgium is concerned, will consider the legislative assemblies of the sub-national entities as 'national parliaments' in the sense of the Constitutional Treaty. In order to implement the Treaty in a way that is compatible with Belgian constitutional law, it is, according to the Council of State, necessary to adapt Belgian domestic law.[48]

In its explanatory note to the draft bill of approval, the *federal government* however put forward the following response to the advisory opinion of the Council of State.[49] According to the federal government, during the intergovernmental conference Belgium intervened to adapt the texts of the subsidiarity protocol and the protocol on national parliaments. The text of the protocols, as originally drafted by the Convention, allegedly excluded explicitly those parliamentary systems that are not unicameral or bicameral.[50] It is a fact that the Convention rejected various (Belgian) amendments that strove for the recognition of the competent regional assemblies within the early warning system.[51]

Article 8 of the protocol on the role of national parliaments as drafted by the Convention stated: 'In the case of bicameral national Parliaments, these provi-

45 Belgian Council of State, section for legislation, opinion 37.978/AV, 15 February 2005, see e.g. Parl. Doc., Senate, 2004-2005, 3-1091/1.

46 Subsidiarity protocol, Article 6.

47 Article 8 of the first protocol (national parliaments); Article 7 (2) of the second protocol (subsidiarity).

48 Parl. Doc., Senate, 2004-2005, 3-1091/1, 541-543.

49 Parl. Doc., Senate, 2004-2005, 3-1091/1, 119-120.

50 Ibid., 113-114; 119-120.

51 See amendments by D. Pieters and the amendments by L. Michel, K. de Gucht, E. di Rupo, A. Van Lancker, P. Chevalier, M. Nagy, P. Dewael to the protocol on the role of the national parliaments and to the protocol on subsidiarity (see CONV 610/1/03 en CONV 611/03).

sions shall apply to both chambers'. In the final text of the Treaty as adopted by the intergovernmental conference, on the other hand, it says: 'Where the national parliamentary system *is not unicameral*, Articles 1 tot 7 shall apply to the component chambers' (emphasis added). Similarly, Article 6 (2) of the protocol on subsidiarity, as drafted by the Convention, stated: 'The national Parliaments of Member States with unicameral Parliamentary systems shall have two votes, while each of the chambers of a bicameral Parliamentary system shall have one vote'. Article 7 (2) of the final text, however, reads: 'Each national Parliament shall have two votes, *shared out on the basis of the national Parliamentary system.* In the case of a bicameral Parliamentary system, each of the two chambers shall have one vote' (emphasis added).

The text adopted by the Convention originally only took into account unicameral and bicameral systems. The final text, by contrast, leaves open what parliamentary systems there are besides a unicameral one, and no longer speaks solely about 'two chambers' but also about 'the component chambers'. Reference is made to the 'national parliamentary system' on the basis of which the votes shall be shared out. For a bicameral parliamentary system a specific rule is laid down, which therefore means that 'national parliamentary system' refers to parliamentary systems other than bicameral ones.

The Belgian federal government claimed that the new reading of the aforementioned Articles is a result of a Belgian intervention.[52] [53] [54] Since it was not possible in the text of the Constitutional Treaty itself to make a reference to the specific characteristics of the Belgian parliamentary system,[55] the texts were amended in an open way and now no longer exclude Belgian specificities. Belgium in this context relied on Article I-5 of the Constitutional Treaty that obliges the European Union to respect the fundamental national constitutional structures.[56] In order to fill in this open character of the protocols, and to avoid

52 Parl. Doc., Senate, 2004-2005, 3-1091/1, 113, 114, 120.

53 In a resolution of 26 February 2004 the European Parliament stated that it supports the early warning system involving national parliaments, and that it believes that, where appropriate, the system should be extended to other parliaments and assemblies within the member states (European Parliament resolution on the Commission report 'Better lawmaking 2002' pursuant to Article 9 of the protocol on the application of the principles of subsidiarity and proportionality (tenth report).

54 According to the 'Report of the general secretariat of the Committee of the Regions, drawn up for the first Conference on Subsidiarity, Berlin, 27 May 2004', the new wording was a result of an amendment at the intergovernmental conference by the Italian presidency 'in order to take account of the specifics of federal structures', CdR 107/2004.

55 In the working group of the Convention on the principle of subsidiarity, a majority of the members considered that the degree of, and arrangements for, the involvement of regional and local authorities in the drafting of Community legislation should be determined solely in the national framework (conclusions of working group I on the principle of subsidiarity, CONV 286/02).

56 Cf. the current Article 6 (3) EU.

any ambiguity, declaration no. 49 was issued. The federal government acknowledged the unilateral character of this declaration but pointed to the fact that the Belgian declaration was not followed by a counter-declaration, which would have been an available means for other member states. Also the government declared that the text of the declaration was drafted after consulting certain 'partners who are sensible to this matter' and with the administration of the Council of Ministers.[57]

4.3 The Internal Co-operation Agreement

Necessity

Whether or not the references in the Constitutional Treaty to 'national parliaments' include Belgian sub-national assemblies, and whether or not the Belgian declaration to that effect is binding upon the EU institutions and other member states, the Council of State and the federal government in any event agreed on the need for internal co-operation agreements at the Belgian domestic level.[58]

With regard to the simplified revision procedure, the Council of State deemed a co-operation agreement *recommendable*, in order to involve the sub-national parliaments in the determination of the position of the national parliament. This involvement would be justified since the revision could lead to changes in stipulations that regulate the exercise of European competencies in the field of matters belonging to regional or community jurisdiction.[59] In the context of the early warning procedure, the Council of State found such a co-operation agreement *necessary*. The involvement of regional and community parliaments as such is necessary given the powers of the sub-national entities and the nature of the envisaged reasoned opinions on subsidiarity which imply a judgment on whether a proposed action cannot be sufficiently achieved by a sub-national authority.[60] This view corresponds with the conclusion of working group IV of the Convention, which stated that national parliaments have a central responsibility to advise, scrutinise, and hold to account, their own government ministers for their performance in the Council, especially when considering whether legislation is best adopted at national or European level.[61] In the Belgian constitutional order, in matters affecting sub-national competences, these parliamentary responsibilities can only be exercised by sub-national assemblies. In fact, their (i.e. sub-national) ministers are establishing

57 Parl. Doc., Senate, 2004-2005, 3-1091/1, 120.

58 Ibid., 114, 120.

59 Ibid., 541.

60 Ibid., 543.

61 Final report of working group IV on the role of national parliaments (CONV 353/02), no. 22.

the Belgian position within the Council, and their ministers are representing Belgium in the Council.[62]

Contents of the co-operation agreement

Despite the uncertain fate of the Constitutional Treaty, negotiations took place in order to reach the mentioned agreement between the Belgian constitutional entities. This was in fact necessary because the Flemish government and the Flemish parliament made the ratification of the Treaty dependent on the conclusion of co-operation agreements.[63] On 19 December 2005 a co-operation agreement implementing the protocol on the application of the principles of subsidiarity and proportionality was concluded between the chairmen of eight parliamentary assemblies.[64]

The negotiations took place in the so-called C7A conference. The C7A is a conference of the chairmen of seven legislative assemblies in Belgium. It involves the two federal chambers, the Flemish parliament, the Walloon parliament, the French community parliament, the parliament of the German-speaking community, and the parliament of the Brussels-Capital region.[65] No

[62] The co-operation agreement of 8 March 1994 deals with the representation of Belgium in the Council of Ministers. The representative of Belgium (and this applies already within Coreper) can only take position in the Council on matters that were subject to a co-ordination procedure. This co-ordination takes place before every meeting of the Council, in the so-called 'Unit European Affairs (P11 or DGE)'. The purpose of the P11 meetings is to transmit instructions to the Belgian ambassador to the EU and to the minister who will represent Belgium in the Council. In case no consensus is reached, the disagreement is brought before the interministerial conference for foreign policy, consisting of ministers themselves, not their representatives. If the conference reaches no common position, Belgium would have to abstain in the Council. The opinion of Belgium has to be defended by its representative. This representative can be a federal, a regional, or a community minister, using the possibility given by Article 203 EC (cf. Article I-23 of the Constitutional Treaty), see also Article 81 (6) of the special institutional reform act. In order to determine who shall be the representative of Belgium, the meetings of the Council are divided into six categories. If the Council deals with exclusively federal matters, Belgium is represented by a federal minister (I). If the Council deals with matters falling mainly within the federal scope of powers, the federal minister is assisted by a regional or community minister representing the sub-national entities (II). If matters are involved for which the sub-national entities are mainly competent, Belgium will be represented by a community or regional minister, assisted by a federal minister (III). And if the Council deals with matters that are exclusively sub-national, Belgium will be represented by a community or regional minister (IV). In order to determine which of the regions or communities designates the representative minister, a half-yearly rotation system is installed. In matters for which only the Flemish region is competent, i.e. fisheries (V), as well as in agricultural matters (VI), Belgium is represented by a federal minister, assisted by both the ministers of the Flemish and the Walloon region.

[63] See footnote 29 *supra*.

[64] Parl. Doc., Flemish Parliament, 2005-06, 628/1.

[65] The assemblies of the French community commission (COCOF) and the joint community commission are no members of this conference. Nevertheless, the discussed procedures of the Constitutional Treaty will apply to them. The co-operation agreement of 19 December 2005 was co-signed by the chairman of the assembly of the COCOF.

governments were participating in these negotiations; the parliaments considered the early warning system to be a purely parliamentary matter in which the governments should not be involved.[66] As a result, the reached agreement has a 'sui generis' character. This kind of inter-parliamentary agreement, bypassing the governments, is a constitutional novelty, and its legal status is uncertain. Moreover, the agreement is only signed by the chairmen of the assemblies, not approved by the assemblies themselves. Only the Flemish parliament approved the agreement in a plenary session.

The agreement regarding the early warning system had to solve three main issues: who would be entitled to issue a reasoned opinion?; how would the interaction between the Belgian parliaments and the Commission and other European institutions be organised?; and how would the two votes of the 'national parliament' be shared out?

The agreement ultimately opted for the principal position following the argument of the federal government regarding declaration no. 49. This means that it is not necessary that the various assemblies reach a common position or a preliminary consensus in order to issue a reasoned opinion on subsidiarity. On the contrary, every assembly is entitled to issue autonomously a reasoned opinion on a perceived violation of the subsidiarity principle.[67] The secretary of the C7A conference will bundle the various opinions, manifesting the origin of each separate opinion. In order to make this system work, given the short six-weeks term determined by Article 6 of the subsidiarity protocol, the co-operation agreement states that the parliaments should receive draft European legislative acts directly from the European institutions. Although the Senate claimed the role of a go-between, it will be the secretary of the C7A, which is de facto a secretary to the chairman of the House of Representatives, who will function as 'postman' with the mentioned limited role of collecting reasoned opinions.

In fact, the co-operation agreement is based on the idea that the main point of the early warning mechanism is the possibility to deliver a reasoned opinion.[68] Once one parliament of a given level has a reasoned objection to a draft European legislative act from the perspective of subsidiarity, this is reason enough to contribute to a possible review by, most notably, the Commission. The availability of two Belgian votes will therefore be reconciled with the idea that all assemblies have the same rights. If one competent assembly issues a reasoned

[66] The chairman of the Flemish parliament specifies that the Constitutional Treaty itself places the subsidiarity scrutiny in the hands of the parliaments (Parl. Doc., Flemish Parliament, 2004-2005, 358/3, 8-9).

[67] This procedure will therefore be fundamentally different from the way a Belgian position in the Council of Ministers is worked out, see footnote 62 *supra*.

[68] According to Kiiver (2006) 36, the early warning system against breaches of subsidiarity under the Constitutional Treaty is based on the counting of incoming complaints from the national parliaments, and the verification whether the number of complaints reached one-third or one-quarter of the votes distributed; nevertheless, the idea that subsidiarity control might raise EU awareness among national parliamentarians in general, as well as other considerations, did play a role as well, ibid., 154-156.

opinion, one of the votes is cast. Only in the case of a draft European legislative act that concerns various levels (federal on the one hand, regional and community on the other hand), each level will be entitled to a maximum of one vote. If the federal authority is involved in the matter that is dealt with in the EU legislative draft, the federal parliament will be able to cast one vote; the other vote goes to the remaining assemblies, which means that each of them can trigger a Belgian non-compliance vote. If the draft act concerns a purely federal matter, the two votes are shared out to the House and the Senate. If the matter is purely regional, the regions have two votes at their disposal. The same goes for matters of pure community competence, respectively. Since there are three regions and three communities, and five assemblies dealing with community matters, the two Belgian votes will be cast if two assemblies object to the European draft – first come, first served. However, the two votes can only be used by two parliaments of different language groups. These language groups are the Dutch one (the Flemish parliament which is a regional as well as a community parliament), the French one (the French community parliament, the Walloon parliament and the French community commission assembly), the German one (the parliament of the German-speaking community) and the bilingual one (the parliament of the Brussels-Capital region and the joint assembly of the joint community commission). If a draft act concerns both regional and community matters, the same rule applies and each language group has the possibility to cast one of the two votes.

The basic option for the equality of each parliament, and their quality of executing the subsidiarity scrutiny, implies also that every parliament can request to bring an action on grounds of an infringement of the principle of subsidiarity before the European Court of Justice. The question whether this action has to be brought by the federal government, or whether parliaments themselves are competent to do so, remains unresolved in the co-operation agreement. It is clear that this system of participation of the various parliaments depends on the possibility to determine, within a very short period of time, which internal competencies are affected by a European draft act. The co-operation agreement recognises the possibility of conflicts with regard to the allocation of powers, and charges the Council of State with the task of giving an advice on this issue within five days.[69]

Remarkably, the agreement does not deal with the position of the 'national parliament' in the context of the simplified treaty revision procedure under Article IV-444 of the Constitutional Treaty, which can be vetoed by any one national parliament or chamber. The Flemish government however insisted that all Belgian parliaments act as chambers of the national parliament in this procedure.[70] Apparently the subsidiarity scrutiny mechanism was considered more urgent, since it can be implemented to a certain extent even without the Consti-

69 This role of the Council of State requires however an amendment of its organic legislation.

70 Parl. Doc., Flemish Parliament, 2004-2005, 358/1, 30.

tutional Treaty entering into force. The simplified revision procedure, on the other hand, depends entirely on the fate of the Constitutional Treaty. Anyway, an agreement on the parliamentary veto in the simplified revision procedure could not be reached in the short term. As a matter of fact, the federal government had fundamental objections to the possibility of a parliamentary veto against the procedure in the first place.[71] A system in which every Belgian assembly would be able to trigger the national blocking power would then be perceived to be even more hazardous than a purely federal veto. It can therefore be expected that an agreement on this point will be worked out in close co-operation with the governments, and it seems all but certain that such an agreement would opt for the same basic option of separate action as the agreement on the early warning system did.

The co-operation agreement: outlook

It is striking to see that the internal Belgian co-operation agreement, although formally it will only enter into force together with the EU Constitutional Treaty, already obliges the parliaments in Belgium to take appropriate measures in order to organise their control mechanisms regarding the respect of the principle of subsidiarity. It is not quite clear what the precise scope of this commitment is, but it seems that it is not impossible that Belgian parliaments, both federal and sub-national, will start to send reasoned opinions on subsidiarity to the European institutions already before the Treaty's entry into force. It is uncertain how the European institutions, in particular the Commission, will respond to the basic principle of the agreement, namely that federal, regional and community assemblies are equal and may adopt independent objections. Since the various reasoned opinions will be actually transmitted by one common go-between, the secretary of the conference of seven assembly chairmen, there will probably be no problem in taking into account these opinions. If one day the early warning procedure of the Constitutional Treaty would enter into force, some more delicate questions will have to be resolved, though. Will the Commission agree to send its drafts directly to all Belgian assemblies, including the sub-national ones? Will the Commission, in line with the internal Belgian co-operation agreement, accept the reasoned opinion of a regional parliament as one negative vote, in the sense of Article 7 of the subsidiarity protocol? Or will the Commission refer to Article 6, arguing that a national parliament may consult regional assemblies where appropriate, but that the negative opinion itself has to be cast by the federal parliament only?

The co-operation agreement leaves more issues unresolved, such as questions of concrete application, the parliamentary blocking powers in the simplified revision procedure, or the access to the European Court of Justice. It is nevertheless an important political precedent. It confirms 'without any reservation' the content of the Belgian final act declaration no. 49, according to which

[71] See footnote 40 *supra*.

federal and sub-national assemblies all form part of one composite national parliament, and the commitment of all Belgian parliaments involved to respect this declaration 'in a spirit of federal loyalty'. Although its legal nature is obscure, the existence of a purely inter-parliamentary agreement indicates the will of the parliaments the take the subsidiarity control into their own hands, without interference from the governments. Whether this parliamentary will can survive political reality is however doubtful.

5 Conclusion

Whether or not final act declaration no. 49 on the co-equal status of federal and sub-national assemblies in Belgium is accepted by the European institutions and the other member states, it is quite evident that it solely reflects Belgian political and constitutional reality. In other words, Belgium has no other option, *rebus sic stantibus*, than to consider 'national parliaments' to mean all its parliaments that are vested with exclusive legislative powers. Belgium therefore cannot but fully fulfil the endeavour of the Committee of the Regions to achieve that regional parliaments with legislative powers act 'as components of the parliamentary machinery in their country or as chambers of the national parliament'.[72] The equal and coordinate position of all Belgian assemblies is demonstrated in the process of the Convention that led to the adoption of the Constitutional Treaty in the first place, in the ratification process, and in the substantive procedures of the Constitutional Treaty itself. The debate on the meaning of the term 'national parliament' also illustrates the fact that in the context of Belgian federalism, the regions and communities, especially the Flemish community, put a lot of effort in developing strategies to bypass the federal level, and to become players of their own right at the European and international level.[73] The described parliamentary co-operation agreement clearly contributes to the pursuit of this goal.

---

72 Opinion of the Committee of the Regions, 'The role of regional parliaments with legislative powers in the democratic life of the Union', 16 November 2005 (CdR 221/2004 fin CONST-023).

73 Bursens (2002) 577.

References

- A. Alen, 'Nationalism – Federalism – Democracy. The Example of Belgium', *Revue européenne de droit public* (1993) 54-58.
- A. Alen and R. Ergec, *Federal Belgium after the fourth state reform of 1993* (Brussels 1998).
- A. Alen and P. Peeters, 'The competences of the Communities in the Belgian Federal State: The Principle of Exclusivity Revisited', *European Public Law* (1997) 170.
- A. Alen and P. Peeters, 'Federal Belgium within the international legal order: theory and practice', in K. Wellens (ed.), *International Law: Theory and Practice*, (The Hague 1998).
- P. Bursens, 'Belgium's Adaptation to the EU. Does Federalism Constrain Europeanisation?', *Res Publica* (2002) 575-597.
- P. Bursens, 'Het Europese beleid in de Belgische federatie. Standpuntbepaling en vertegenwoordiging van de Belgische belangen', *Res Publica* (2005) 58-79.
- F. Delmartino, 'Belgium after the fourth state reform: completed federalism or federalism in the making?', in G. Färber and M. Forsyth (eds), *The Regions – Factors of Integration or Disintegration in Europe?* (Baden-Baden 1996).
- T. Delreux, *Political implications on the EU Constitutional Treaty: a process-oriented approach of the Belgian case*, IIEB Working Paper no. 14, 2005.
- K. Deschouwer, 'Kingdom of Belgium', in J. Kincaid and A. Tarr (eds), *A Global Dialogue on Federalism. Volume 1. Constitutional origins, structure, and change in federal countries* (Montreal 2005).
- F. Goudappel, *Powers and Control Mechanisms in European Federal Systems* (Deventer 1998).
- F. Ingelaere, *Een verkenning van de Europese Grondwet en van het meerlaagse bestuur in de Europese Unie* (Brugge 2005).
- Ph. Kiiver, *The National Parliaments in the European Union. A Critical View on EU Constitution-Building* (The Hague 2006).
- J.V. Louis and A. Alen, 'La constitution et la participation à la communauté européenne', *Revue belge de Droit International* (1994) 81-109.
- W. Pas, 'A dynamic federalism built on static principles: The Belgian Case', in A. Tarr, R. Williams and J. Marko (eds), *Federalism, Subnational Constitutions, and Minority Rights* (London 2004).
- P. Peeters, 'Federalism: a comparative perspective – Belgium transforms from a unitary to a federal state', in B. De Villiers (ed.), *Evaluating Federal Systems* (Dordrecht 1994).
- R. Vuillermoz, *La Belgique, l'Espagne et l'Italie face à l'intégration communautaire* (Brussels 2003).
- J. Wouters and L. De Smet, 'The Legal Position of Federal States and Their Federated Entities in International Relations', in T. Vandamme and J. Reestman (eds), *Ambiguity in the Rule of Law. The Interface between National and International Legal Systems* (Groningen 2001).

CHAPTER 6

The Dutch Parliament and the European Constitution

How Yes led to No

Olaf Tans

1 Introduction

In the Netherlands, the negative outcome of the referendum on the EU Constitutional Treaty has caused confusion about the nation's attitude towards the European Union. On the one hand, it is hard to believe that the Dutch openness and pragmatism with regard to international co-operation has really come to an end. This attitude goes back to the very origin of the Dutch state, that was first created, in 1588, as a republic of seven autonomous regions deciding to unite for both military and economic reasons.[1] Ever since that 'golden age', the Dutch have chosen to profit, rather than to close off, from external influences. This is reflected by the fact that the Dutch constitution contains an Article stating that international law is directly applicable and binding in the national legal order, as well as an Article stating that international law is superior to national law.[2] With regard to European integration, the Dutch have always proudly considered themselves to be frontrunners, striving for the most far-reaching agreements, and never afraid to give up sovereignty. On the other hand, the outcome of the referendum on the European Constitutional Treaty speaks for itself: of the 63.3 percent of the electorate that made it to the ballot box, 61.5 percent said 'no'.[3] How is this possible? One explanation is that European integration may be a high priority to the Dutch government, but not necessarily to the Dutch people.[4] Although empirical research indicates that the citizens of the Netherlands and Luxembourg have shown the most stable and loyal attitude towards European integration, it is possible to question the strength of this loyalty.[5] Hoetjes, for example, states that in the Netherlands '...European integration became a matter of "positive indifference"'.[6] The author confirms that Dutch citizens have generally been well disposed to the EU, but stresses that this is not accompanied by much passion. Long ago, they seem to have simply accepted the fact that the EU is a worthy cause, and do not seem to have given it another thought.[7] The issue was entrusted to a specialised elite

1 The seven regions united militarily in order to keep the Spanish army from conquering the Netherlands. Furthermore, they sought to co-ordinate and collectively arrange certain aspects of their overseas trade. In both ways, this co-operation turned out to be a success. See Israel (1995); Rowen and Lossky (1995); Price (1994), as referred to in Van der Pot and Donner (2001) 107.

2 More specifically, Article 93 of the Dutch constitution reads: 'Provisons in treaties and decisions of international organisations that, judging from their content, can bind anyone, are binding after they have been made public.' Article 94 reads: 'Laws that are valid in the Kingdom are not applied if this application is in breach with provisions in treaties and decisions of international organisations that, judging from their content, can bind anyone.'

3 Source: www.europese-grondwet.nl/a/referendum/analyse-uitslag.html.

4 Other explanations of the Dutch 'no' are discussed in: Aarts and Van der Kolk (2006).

5 Janssen (2001) 135, see also Van Schendelen (2004), Van der Eijk and Franklin (1996).

6 Hoetjes (2001) 338.

7 Hoetjes (1996) 155-184.

which presented it – if at all – as a technical and uncontroversial matter. Even during the 1960s and 1970s, when the country went through a period of social change combined with a polarising political climate, European integration was hardly put on the agenda. The Dutch were simply in favour, and left it to the government to make the EU work.

Until the referendum. For the first time the Dutch were asked to actively support a step in the integration process, rather than to let it happen passively, and it turned out that they did not have the required political will. So the nation was left with the question: *what do we want?*

This contribution is premised on the idea that the actual debate on the Dutch attitude towards the EU disregards a vital aspect. The current debate focuses on how the government failed miserably to 'sell' the Constitutional Treaty to the people, stressing the notion that rulers and the ruled are growing ever more apart, that citizens can no longer identify with the way they are governed, let alone with the EU, and that this abstract power is producing regulations that seem to fall down from an immense height. This line of argument, however, seems to close its eyes to a crucial fact, namely that the Netherlands are a representative democracy, and that representative democracies are characterised by the fact that the link between the government and the people is established by means of representative bodies voicing the will of the people. In other words, the main input to political life, the prime expression of what 'we' want, is meant to come from the parliament. Therefore, this contribution focuses on the role of the Dutch parliament in the European constitution-building process. Rather than to point the finger at either the distant government or the unwilling people, we pose an essential question that, for some strange reason, has not been posed very often: *what did the parliament want?*

In the following paragraphs, the attitude of the Dutch parliament *vis-à-vis* the European constitution will be addressed in two ways. Firstly, the attitude of this parliament with regard to the European constitution-building process will be discussed. What were the main contributions and points of discussion with regard to the Convention on the future of Europe, and how has the Dutch parliament dealt with these issues on the way to the referendum? Secondly, the attitude of the Dutch parliament will be discussed on the basis of how it has reacted to its new role, as defined in the protocols attached to the Constitutional Treaty, in particular the role of watchdog of the principles of subsidiarity and proportionality. Finally, an attempt will be made to explain how the Dutch parliament may have played a role in the failed ratification.

2 The Dutch Parliament and the Convention: From Illusion to Disillusion

According to Christian-Democratic MP and substitute Convention member Van Dijk, the Dutch parliament has been much more involved with the European Convention than it is usually involved with EU affairs.[8] Firstly, this must be due to the fact that the organisation of the Convention itself fostered transparency and openness of deliberation, for example by comprising so many different political actors, among which representatives of national parliaments, and by publication of all the official documents, contributions, amendments and records of proceedings on the Convention website.[9] Secondly, the activity of the Dutch parliament was stimulated by intense processes of information and consultation at the national level.[10] However, the fact that the Dutch parliament has been relatively strongly involved with the Convention does not necessarily mean that there has been much political debate. As will be described in the following paragraph, there seems to have been a relatively high level of agreement about the Dutch priorities and strategies to be followed. And when the Convention reached its conclusion, there was a relatively broadly shared feeling of concern and disappointment.[11]

---

8 Jan Jacob van Dijk was a substitute participant of the Convention on behalf of the Dutch parliament, more particularly on behalf of the Christian-Democratic party (CDA). He published several articles with regard to the European constitutional process, for example: Van Dijk (2004), Van Dijk (2005). Some of his opinions are discussed on the basis of an interview that took place on 2 November 2005. Other Dutch representatives in the Convention were: Hans van Mierlo (D66, March-September 2002), Gijs de Vries (VVD, from October 2002 onwards), and Tom de Bruijn (substitute), all on behalf of the government. On behalf of the lower chamber: Frans Timmermans (Social-Democrats), Hans van Baalen (VVD, March-September 2002). On behalf of the upper chamber: René van der Linden (CDA), Wim van Eekelen (VVD, substitute). On behalf of the European Parliament: Hanja Maij-Weggen (CDA).

9 An interesting analysis of this dynamic can be found in MacCormick (2005).

10 The involvement of the Dutch parliament was facilitated, firstly, by a variety of information flows: contributions by the Dutch representatives, mission statements by the government, reports of the Convention's progress and the Dutch contribution by the minister of foreign affairs, a number of contributions by the WRR, a think-tank, and of course the regular reports of parliamentary proceedings and the documents published on the Convention's website. Secondly, the involvement of the Dutch parliament was facilitated by a variety of consultation procedures: meetings of the Dutch representatives and the special committees of European affairs, general meetings of a number of special committees and representatives of the government and parliamentary debates.

11 EU-03-101, EU-03-105.

2.1 A Basic Consensus: Countering Big-Member-State Dominance

From the outset, the Dutch political actors seem to have been united in their opposition to a number of institutional proposals from the presidium of the Convention and some of the bigger member states, which basically aimed at strengthening the position of the European Council, for example by introducing a permanent presidency.[12] According to the Dutch government, there were two main objections to these proposals.[13] Firstly, they would disturb the institutional balance within the EU, mostly at the cost of the power of the European Commission and the influence of small member states. Secondly, the early institutional proposals would decrease the democratic legitimacy of European governance in that the permanent presidency was not designed to be responsible to a representative body.

In order to counter these proposals, the Dutch worked together with Belgium and Luxembourg in launching the so called 'Benelux memorandum'.[14] This contribution stressed the importance of the Community method, and seeks to maintain the balance between the institutions and the equality of the member states. A central feature of the memorandum is that it proposes to strengthen the role of the Commission, starting with the following statement: 'The Commission is the Institution that guarantees the common interest. It is the engine of the European integration. This function will be even more important in an enlarged Union with more numerous and more diverse states. Therefore the Commission needs to be reinforced....'.[15] This reaction to the early institutional proposals by the bigger member states seems to have been supported by a vast majority in the Dutch parliament, and has set the tone for the Dutch voice in the Convention. In a parliamentary debate held in March 2003, all political parties expressed, in one way or the other, a fear of being dominated by the bigger member states, stressing the importance of the rotating chairmanship of the European Council, of the Community method (as opposed to intergovernmentalist tendencies) and of institutional balance within the EU.[16] At the end of this debate, the secretary of state of foreign affairs strikingly illustrated the atmosphere by referring to the 'sun king proposals' of France, Germany and other countries, and by concluding that almost all speakers had expressed their concern about them.

---

[12] The framework presented by chairman Giscard d'Estaing, the French/German and the British/Spanish institutional proposals.

[13] TK 2002-2003, 28473, nr. 4, p. 8.

[14] CONV 457/02. Presented at the lower chamber of the Dutch parliament on 5 December 2002.

[15] CONV 457/02, p. 3. The memorandum proposes, for example: (1) to have a Commission President elected by the European Parliament; (2) to have a strong and in numbers reduced Commission; (3) to give the Commission the exclusive right of initiative in legislative matters.

[16] TK 49/3237-3265, 13 March 2003.

Of course other points have been raised as well. The role of national parliaments, for example, was discussed by a number of parties. Interestingly, the most left-wing party, the Socialist Party, was the most passionate in stressing the importance of national parliamentary control to counterbalance the undemocratic aspects of the EU, notably the dominance of the European Council, whereas the major right-wing party, the VVD, was of the opinion that national parliaments should not be entitled to directly affect the EU, as this political community was designed to be legitimised and controlled by the European Parliament. Furthermore, in the sphere of basic principles and values, it was claimed that a European constitution should not refer to the Charter of fundamental rights, and that it should contain some reference to Christian values. Finally, it may not be irrelevant that a number of parties expressed a certain sense of being taken by surprise by the fact that the Convention had turned out to be such an ambitious undertaking, seeking to redesign the entire institutional make-up of the EU, whereas it had started in a rather explorative manner.

2.2 Disappointment and Concern about the Outcome of the Convention

Towards the end of the Convention, when its result started to become visible, the initial confidence (or was it recklessness?) gave way to a rather worried and critical atmosphere in and around the Dutch parliament. One of the Dutch representatives in the Convention, for example, published an article in a newspaper entitled: 'Holland cannot accept this constitution'. The article claims that the draft Treaty establishes the dominance of the 'Big Five', and that this was covered up by an optically delusive strengthening of the position of the Commission and the European Parliament. Giscard d'Estaing played the game very well, by consciously asking too much, by deliberately provoking and then making concessions. In the end, however, he has exactly achieved what he wanted.[17]

Being aware of the historical importance of the decision-making process lying ahead, it was decided to organise something unique: a joint meeting of a number of standing committees of both the upper and the lower chamber of the Dutch parliament, and the government. Up until then, such meetings had only taken place with regard to a declaration of war or approval of a royal marriage. At the opening, on 10 June 2003, a spokesman of the Christian-Democratic party proudly declared that a precedent was being created, which turned out to be true, as will be discussed later on. During this joint meeting, some did their best to see the positive aspects of the Convention's progress, but that does not weigh up to the many utterances of disappointment and frustration.[18] MP Van Dijk, for example, started out by appreciating the fact that Article 2 of the

[17] J.C. van Baalen in the *N.R.C.*, summer 2003.

[18] TK 2002-2003, 28473, 158e and 33.

draft Treaty acknowledges that, apart from being a pragmatic mode of co-operation, the EU is also a community based on certain values. Furthermore, he was positive about the increased competence of the European Parliament and the exclusive right of initiative granted to the Commission. With regard to the European Council, however, Van Dijk stated to have 'a lot of trouble' dealing with the power attributed to this institution, and with the risk of more bureaucracy. These elements, he stressed, are a cause for great concern. Convention member and Social-Democratic MP Timmermans claimed that the Convention was actually progressing quite well, yet this positivism is not very convincing given the fact that it was embedded in a fierce criticism of the government's attitude with regard to the Convention, an attitude characterised by '...bad judgement, wrong bidding, too late and too little...'.[19] A spokesman of the liberal-democratic party, D66, expressed a similar criticism by wondering whether the government had operated on the basis of any strategy at all.

In hindsight, however, the most interesting aspect of this parliamentary debate was the growing realisation of the fact that society was hardly interested in the matter. More precisely, the members of parliament seemed to become aware of the fact that the Dutch positive indifference, which was mentioned in the introduction to this contribution, was turning into a state of negative indifference. The Green party, for example, deplored that the Convention had not yet led to a significant public debate. The Socialist Party in fact argued that the democratic support for a transferral of competences 'from The Hague to Brussels' had rather diminished than grown over the last few years. The Social-Democrat Timmermans, finally, seems to have hit the nail on the head by stating that the Dutch seemed to conceive of Europe similar to the way they conceive of the weather: it can be good, it is mostly bad, but either way nothing can be done about it.

Even more striking is a point made by a member of the upper chamber indicating that the Dutch parliament itself suffered from the same indifference. This member, the Social-Democrat Jurgens, signalled that the parliamentary debate about the Convention was held in the margin of deliberations on a rather trivial governmental policy statement, whereas it would have been more appropriate to give the centre stage to an issue such as a draft Treaty establishing a Constitution for Europe. As Jurgens remarked, however, this is quite indicative of the Dutch parliament's attitude. 'It is typical...,' he added, '...that as soon Europe is discussed the listeners leave the room.'[20]

---

19 TK 2002-2003, 28473, 158e and 33, p. 9.

20 TK 2002-2003, 28473, 158e and 33, p. 11.

3 The Path to the Referendum: How to Sell a Half-Empty Glass?

After its primary reaction of disappointment and concern, having to deal with the disillusion of being the assembly of a small member state lacking the power to significantly influence the constitution-building process, the Dutch parliament quickly regrouped. Instead of revelling in a sense of defeat, it shifted to a more realistic and pragmatic attitude. However disappointing the outcome of the Convention – and later the intergovernmental conference – may have been, now it had to be decided whether this outcome was to be preferred to having no outcome at all. This rapid change of attitude may have been informed by a growing awareness among the members of parliament that they might well turn out to have a crucial role. In 2003, a bill was proposed according to which the Constitutional Treaty would be submitted to a referendum.[21] If that bill would pass, which in fact happened in January 2005, it would mean that the voice of the people would become vital, and that political parties would have an important share in guiding the people in its voting behaviour. In other words, the parliament seemed to develop a sense of responsibility for the eventual Dutch position with regard to the Constitutional Treaty.

3.1 Closing the Parliamentary Ranks after the IGC

This change of attitude is expressed in the parliamentary debate on the outcome of the intergovernmental conference.[22] MP Van Baalen, who had been very critical on other occasions, opened this debate by stating: 'Chairman. The question is: is the glass half full or half empty?' He moved on by repeating some of the earlier doubts of his right-of-centre VVD party, and then stated that 'what is done is done', and that the parliament must decide whether the Constitutional Treaty was an improvement compared to the Treaty of Nice. Van Baalen concluded that, although a number of Dutch priorities have not been realised, the glass was still half-full and that the Constitutional Treaty deserved parliamentary support.

Not surprisingly, this opening argument provoked the criticism that the VVD party was like a barking dog that never bites. In fairness, however, one must conclude that the VVD was not alone in this. Judging from the statements by their spokesmen, over 85% of the Dutch parliament was now in favour of the outcome of the intergovernmental conference. The two other coalition parties, the Christian-Democrats and the liberal-democratic D66, both declared to be positive about it, notwithstanding the fact that some aspects could have been better, and that they were going to advise the Dutch people to say 'yes' to the Constitutional Treaty. Even the main opposition party, the Social-Democratic

---

[21] TK 2002-2003, 28885, nr.1-3, 22 May 2003.

[22] TK 87/5555-5587, 23 June 2004.

Party, was very cheerful: 'It may be strange...,' said MP Timmermans, '...that a representative of the opposition is saying this, for up till now my colleagues have not done so, but I want to congratulate the prime-minister wholeheartedly with the result he has achieved. To the Netherlands and to Europe it is clearly a step ahead.'[23]

Given the outcome of the referendum, one cannot disregard the opinions of the small group of parties opposed to the Constitutional Treaty, consisting of the Socialist Party, the party of the murdered right-wing populist Pim Fortuyn, and the small Christian parties CU and SGP. The spokesman of the Socialists repeated the criticism which this party had had all along: the Constitutional Treaty establishes the dominance of bigger member states and is an expression of neo-liberal ideology, based on the idea of competition in all domains, without making a distinction between the private and the public sphere. The Fortuyn party argued that the Constitutional Treaty illustrates the over-regulating and boundless character of the EU, and that it would only lead to more bureaucracy. Interestingly, a spokesman of this party later declared to be surprised by the fact that the bill of approval of the Constitutional Treaty had been introduced prior to the date of the referendum, and stressed that this might be interpreted by the voters as a sign of arrogance.[24] The leader of one of the Christian parties, finally, also deplored that the Constitutional Treaty led to 'more Brussels' and that the preamble contained an unbalanced reference to cultural, religious and humanist traditions. His main point, however, was that the lack of social support for the project Europe made the Constitutional Treaty a bridge too far, too soon.

3.2 The Campaign and the Unfavourable Social Climate

In the aftermath of the referendum, the government was criticised for launching a pathetic campaign, but it is doubtful whether that is true, and whether a good campaign, whatever that may be, would have made any difference.

The campaign roughly comprised an information and a persuasion phase. In the first phase, the people were informed about the Constitutional Treaty by means of television features, leaflets, websites, all seeking to discuss the complicated matter in simple terms. At this point, in spring 2005, the first opinion polls indicated that there was no majority among the Dutch people to support the Constitutional Treaty. In the second phase, ministers would appear on television to say that the Treaty really was a good thing, and that a Dutch 'no' would spell disaster, but for some reason this only made things worse. When the polls continued to be negative, leaders of political parties joined the campaign, but again public opinion was remarkably unimpressed. Moreover, it must be

23 TK 87/5563, 23 June 2004.

24 TK 2004-2005, 30025 (R1783), nr. 6, p. 4. The bill of approval (TK 2004-2005, 30025, nr. 1) was passed in March 2005, whereas the referendum was held in June 2005.

noted that the parties opposed to the Constitutional Treaty launched a much more aggressive campaign. One member of the Socialist Party attracted a lot of attention by making bold statements, and by sailing through Amsterdam's canals on a boat full of 'no' signs, thus creating an atmosphere where it was fun to go against the government and the big parties. A dissident member of the VVD rented a bus and travelled through the country for two weeks. Even the small Christian parties, not known for an aggressive style, acquired a taste for it and started to actively campaign against the Constitutional Treaty. In this light, the statements by the government and the leading parties sounded somewhat perfunctory and sometimes even patronising, as if they were still not able to imagine the electorate actually rebelling.

Most detrimental to the pro-campaign, however, was an exceptionally unfavourable social climate, characterised by pessimism and confusion. In 2005, the Dutch economy went through a nearly unprecedented crisis that had already led to major budget cuts and sacrifices. Moreover, public opinion started to become convinced of the idea that the euro had led to drastic rises in prices, and of the idea that the government had made errors when the common currency was introduced. Furthermore, the Netherlands had just seen the brutal murder of the controversial film-maker Theo van Gogh by an Islamic fundamentalist, which caused a shock and rekindled the type of social tensions that had earlier been aroused by the murder of the politician Pim Fortuyn: mistrust in the regular order of things, mostly in the political establishment. Worst of all, the government was led by the Christian-Democratic prime-minister Balkenende, who was widely considered to lack charisma and authority. The country did not only miss leadership, but also had to deal with confronting the question why this strange character – with the nickname Harry Potter in reference to his visual resemblance to the young wizard apprentice – was put in that position and why he was able to stay there.

In this social climate, so it seems, the Dutch electorate would have voted off many proposals, no matter how full the glass, simply because it felt the need to say 'no'. It simply did not want to have ministers and members of parliament tell them what to do, or rather, it *did* want them to do so, and then ridicule and ignore it. It was fed up by the crises, had lost 'its innocence' and wanted to revolt. Finally, it may not be irrelevant that the French had said 'no' prior to the Dutch referendum, thus making it much easier to be a spoilsport.

4 Anticipating the Role of Guardian of Subsidiarity and Proportionality

Meanwhile, the attitude of the Dutch parliament *vis-à-vis* the European constitution-building process was already being tested in a different way. Apart from contributing to the democratic legitimacy of the Constitutional Treaty, national parliaments also started to anticipate their role as defined within this institutional framework: their role as 'watchdog' of the principles of subsidiarity and proportionality.[25] This may appear to be somewhat rash, but we must keep in mind that the national parliamentary competence to test EU decision-making on these principles was already established in the Treaty of Amsterdam. As we shall see, in the last few years the Dutch parliament has been energetic in putting that competence to practice.

4.1 The Joint Committee on the Application of Subsidiarity

As mentioned, the Dutch parliamentary debate with regard to the Convention led to a novelty: joint meetings of standing committees of both the upper and the lower chamber, and members of the cabinet.[26] These meetings were characterised by strong arguments and utterances of disappointment, but most speakers were positive about one thing: the protocols on subsidiarity and proportionality. Therefore, both chambers passed a motion asking for the establishment of a temporary committee composed of members of both chambers, with the task to find out how the Dutch parliament was to play its role as indicated in these protocols.[27] This joint committee on the application of subsidiarity, another novelty in Dutch parliamentary history, was established in November 2003.[28]

In order to come up with a solid advice, this temporary committee asked a number of experts to interpret the protocols. Furthermore, a questionnaire was sent to all the national parliaments of the EU to find out how they were preparing for their role as guardians of the principles of subsidiarity and proportionality. Finally, a meeting with representatives of 'civil society' and regional governments was organised. In its advice, the joint committee first remarked that European integration had a significant impact on the Dutch legal order, but that many politicians are only confronted with it after decision-making has already taken place in the Council, and that an early subsidiarity check could be an improvement in this respect. Interestingly, the committee did not only present this as a solution to an external institutional problem, but also as a remedy to an internal mentality problem: by effectuating the early warning system, members of parliament would no longer be able to disregard the European decision-making process. According to the joint committee this is an important purpose of the protocols. European legislation should no longer be dominated by a select group of specialists, but should rather become a part of every parlamentarian's daily work.

---

[25] Peters (2005) 70-72.

[26] This paragraph is to a considerable extent based on Van Dijk (2005).

[27] TK 2002-2003, 28473, nr. 13 (Motion Van Dijk c.s.); EK 2002-2003, 28473, nr. 158G (Motion Van de Beeten c.s.).

[28] This committee consisted of four members of each chamber. Chairman was J.J. van Dijk.

Starting from that premise, the committee proposed to install a standing committee on subsidiarity, composed of members of the upper and the lower chamber.[29] Two arguments were put forward. Firstly, a permanent joint committee was needed for efficiency reasons, namely to be able to finalise a judgment within the period of six weeks mentioned in the protocols. Secondly, a permanent joint committee would increase the chance of reaching unanimity among the two chambers, which was deemed necessary to have a significant influence on European decision-making. It was proposed, and accepted by both chambers in December 2004, that the standing committee on subsidiarity would function as follows. Its general task would be to determine whether proposals by the European Commission are in accordance with the principles of subsidiarity and proportionality. In order to make that judgment, the standing committee would distribute EU proposals among the sectoral committees with the request to give their opinion within three weeks. The standing committee would give its advice on the basis of these opinions, and send it to both chambers of the parliament, which could decide to vote on them. As this procedure puts a lot of pressure on the members of parliament, social organisations and local governments, it was proposed that legislative proposals would be published on a website and in the government gazette, and that social organisations were to be informed via e-mail. In sum, this procedure was meant to foster participation of both the parliament and civil society, as well as transparency.

It is not yet entirely clear how this works out in practice. In March 2005, COSAC, the European Union's inter-parliamentary conference, launched an experiment in which national parliaments were asked to scrutinise a number of proposals by the Commission.[30] Following the aforementioned procedure, the Dutch joint committee passed the proposals on to sectoral committees of both chambers of parliament. It turned out that these sectoral committees scrutinised the proposals in rather different manners, and that they came up with two completely different opinions.[31] The joint committee decided to organise a meeting with the purpose to arrive at a consistent and unanimous advice, which took quite a bit of argument.

---

29 More specifically, it was proposed to allow a seat in the committee to every party with more that 20 seats in the lower chamber or ten seats in the upper chamber, and to every party represented in both chambers.

30 Conférence des Organes Specialisés en Affaires Communautaires. The proposals can be found in: E040148-E040152/COM(2004)140-144. The experiment is discussed in Kiiver (2006) 158-161.

31 The standing committee of the upper chamber gathered a few times, operating mostly as a team. In the lower chamber, the process got more politicised: much work was done by separate political groups, which also got in touch with their party members in the European Parliament. It was remarkable that the standing committees of the upper and the lower chamber did not get in touch with each other.

4.2 Pulling it Through in Spite of the Failed Ratification

After the French and Dutch referendums it was decided to answer the European Council's call for 'a period of reflection' by taking a break to reconsider the plan to install a permanent joint committee. It appeared, however, that the Dutch parliament was still very supportive: even the parties that had campaigned against the Constitutional Treaty wanted to examine the possibilities to realise the subsidiarity and proportionality check. One of the considerations was that this would meet the concern of the Dutch people that 'Europe' was developing too fast and uncontrolled. Furthermore, it was argued that although the protocols would not be ratified, the Treaty of Amsterdam provided a legal basis for the subsidiarity and proportionality check, and that it was in fact negligent that the national parliaments of the EU had not yet acted upon it.

Hence, the temporary joint committee resumed its activities. It shared the opinion that a Union-wide approach was to be preferred because that would have a greater impact on the European Commission. Therefore, it was suggested that COSAC should take the matter in hands and propose a procedure for a subsidiarity and proportionality check by national parliaments in the EU. In October 2005, the UK presidency of COSAC proposed such a procedure.[32] In December 2005 the temporary joint committee gave its final advice, basically stating that the permanent committee should take over and organise its activities in accordance with the COSAC line.[33] Although members of the lower chamber expressed a few doubts about this advice in a plenary debate, it was decided that the standing committee on subsidiarity would start to function in January 2006.[34]

5 Characterising the Attitude of the Dutch Parliament

On the basis of the foregoing, one cannot derive one coherent characterisation of the attitude of the Dutch parliament with regard to the EU Constitutional Treaty. Rather, we have to conclude that this parliament has shown a variety of attitudes, which will be sketched below. An attempt will also be made to add something to the story of the failed ratification.

5.1 Consensus, Co-operation and Support

First of all, the foregoing analysis seems to reflect some characteristics of the so-called consensus democracy.[35] Although the parliamentary debate with regard to the Constitutional Treaty shows a large number of little

---

32 See www.cosac.org/en/meetings/previous/London2005/oedinary/meetingdocuments.

33 TK 2005-2006, 30389, nr. 1.

34 TK 15 December 2005.

35 Lijphart (1999) 31-47.

disagreements, it is striking that many members of the Dutch parliament seemed to agree on major issues on various occasions. From the very outset, for example, the parliament seems to have been motivated by a widespread fear of being dominated by the big member states, a fear that was voiced in a unanimous opposition to the permanent presidency of the European Council, and in massive support for the idea to strengthen the European Commission. When the intergovernmental conference reached its final stage, the Dutch parliament was largely disappointed about the outcome. When the referendum approached, finally, the main political parties seemed to unite in their attempt to take responsibility and to sell the Constitutional Treaty to the sceptical Dutch voters.

Moreover, we can say that the consensus was to a considerable extent supportive of the opinions and actions of those directly involved in the constitution-building process. In other words, the government and a vast majority of the parliament seem to have formed a unity in their approach to the European constitution-building process. This confirms a widely recognised development of the Dutch parliamentary system, namely a 'monistic' tendency.[36] Rather than opposing each other, the government and the coalition parties tend to collaborate on the basis of a coalition agreement. This tendency is often considered to lead to a new dualism between the government and coalition parties, on the one hand, and the opposition parties, on the other. In the case of the European constitution-building process, however, even the main opposition party seems to have been part of the block supporting the government, respectively the Dutch representatives. This is not to say that the Dutch parliament has been the subject of extreme executive dominance. The foregoing analysis rather shows that the parliament seems to have affected the Dutch position *vis-à-vis* the European constitution-building process by engaging in a wide variety of mainly informal contacts with influential political actors, notably the Dutch representatives in the Convention and the government. Conversely, it can be noted that these political actors in turn have informal means to influence what is going on in the parliament. In short, we witness a political culture of 'consultation' that is typical for consociational democracies, and that is characterised by an intertwined and mutually dependent relation between executive and legislative power.[37]

5.2 Pragmatism and Political Passivity

This type of executive-legislative relation has been cherished for a number of reasons. In sociological terms it relies heavily on self-organisation: unregulated mechanisms of interest articulation, deliberation and decision-making that are considered to yield stability, predictability and – last but not least – the ability to produce practical results. The latter is illustrated by the

36 For example in Andeweg (1991).

37 Holzhacker (2004) provides some support to this analysis by observing that the Dutch parliamentary practice is relatively unregulated in comparison to the German and the Danish polities.

activity of the Dutch parliament with regard to the proportionality and subsidiarity check. By means of a finely-tuned interaction between relevant groups, also taking the opinion of government and external experts into consideration, it turned out to be possible to introduce a novelty in Dutch parliamentary history. There is, however, also a downside to this type of parliamentary behaviour, which becomes clear by simply looking at the figures: 85 percent of the parliament supported a treaty that was rejected by over 61 percent of the voters. This means that although there was a considerable level of agreement in the Dutch parliament, and a preparedness to act upon it, this did not reflect the opinion of the electorate. This raises the question whether the parliament performed its representative function well. It appears to have lost track of the voter by focusing on its internal consensus-oriented political process. This phenomenon has been observed in various ways. The murdered politician Pim Fortuyn, for example, used the term 'old politics' to refer to the mechanisms by which the political establishment sustains its power. This led to a public debate about the gap between the government and the citizens. In relation to the Belgian parliamentary democracy, others have observed consociationalism leading to 'elite-driven' political decision-making, and low levels of political participation.[38] The Dutch coalition parties supporting the second Balkenende cabinet have recognised a similar problem, and have decided to co-operate on the basis of a tiny coalition agreement in order to leave more room for political input during the four-year period of government.

The parliamentary debates about the Constitutional Treaty reveal a factor that may be even more detrimental to the parliament's representative function, namely political passivity. It is striking that although the Constitutional Treaty became a matter of great concern to a select group of members of parliament, it remained a matter of little importance to the majority of the parliament, just like other EU affairs are. More importantly, the parliamentary debates show passivity in the sense that the Constitutional Treaty has not given rise to major political conflicts. One may argue that this is a positive consequence of consensus-building, but in the light of the failed ratification one can also argue that herein lies the core of the problem. By engaging in conflict, namely, a parliament makes clear that there is something at stake, and that differences of opinion are possible. If voters can relate to one of these opinions that will generate a sense of being represented, and an impression of a political arena in which interests and preferences are played out.[39] The parliamentary treatment of the Constitutional Treaty, however, remained rather flat and pragmatic. Even in the final stages of the campaign, the government and the main political parties produced little more than the unanimous message that it was important to say 'yes', mainly because that would not jeopardise the further development of the EU. No seri-

[38] Walgrave et al. (2004).

[39] The issue of political representation with regard to the EU constitutional progress is discussed in Crum (2005).

ous attempt was made to discuss why Holland would be in favour of this further development. In other words, the European constitutional ambition was hardly politicised.

6 Conclusion

In the light of the Dutch 'no' to the EU Constitutional Treaty, this contribution has examined the attitude of the Dutch parliament with regard to the European constitution-building process. This attitude has been analysed on the basis of the parliamentary debates concerning the Convention, the development of these debates, the campaign on the way to the referendum, and finally the parliamentary activities in relation to the role of national parliaments in controlling EU decision-making as defined in the protocol on the principles of subsidiarity and proportionality. Drawing from more general theories about (former) consociational democracies, the attitude of the Dutch parliament has been characterised as consensus-oriented, co-operative, and relatively supportive of the actions and opinions of those directly involved in the European constitution-building process. Furthermore, one cannot take away from the Dutch parliament its capacity – albeit in this co-operative style – to exert influence, generate political support, and make things happen through mainly informal channels. The proactive behaviour of the Dutch parliament in putting the subsidiarity check to practice serves as a good illustration of this capacity.

The disparity between parliamentary and electoral support for the Constitutional Treaty however must lead to a more critical tone. It indicates that there is not only a gap between Dutch citizens and their government, but also – or even notably – between Dutch citizens and their representatives in the parliament, at least where the European constitution-building process is concerned. This contribution suggests that the style of parliamentary debate may be a causal factor. Like most EU affairs, the Constitutional Treaty was discussed in a rather uninspired and technical manner, without many fundamental differences of opinion. This is detrimental to the catalysing role a parliament can play in public debate, and its potency to politicise issues and thereby to inspire the people to a certain political engagement.

Ending on a positive note, it may be worth mentioning that the Dutch 'no' may yet have had a positive effect. MP Van Dijk observes a remarkably increased EU awareness among the Dutch members of parliament. They used to leave it up to the specialists to deal with EU affairs, but they seem to have realised that early intervention is necessary to have influence. According to Van Bommel of the Socialist Party, the Dutch 'no' has also had a positive effect on the EU itself: legislative proposals are withdrawn more frequently, and existing regulation is reviewed more critically.[40] It seems the EU is finally learning to constrain its own activities.

[40] TK 15 December 2005.

References

- K. Aarts and H. van der Kolk, 'Understanding the Dutch "No": the Euro, the East, and the Elite', *Political Science and Politics* (2006), forthcoming.
- R.B. Andeweg, 'Volksvertegenwoordiging en regering', in J.J.A. Thomassen, *Hedendaagse democratie* (Alphen aan den Rijn 1991).
- J.C. van Baalen, 'Nederland mag deze grondwet niet accepteren', in *N.R.C.*, 19 June 2003.
- B. Crum, *The EU Constitutional Process: A Failure of Political Representation?*, paper presented at the annual work-conference of the Netherlands Institute for Government, Nijmegen 2005.
- J.J. van Dijk, 'Juist zonder Europese grondwet een subsidiariteitstoets', in: *Internationale Spectator* (2005) 654-659.
- J.J. van Dijk, 'De wordingsgeschiedenis van de grondwet voor Europa: een kritische terugblik', *Christen Democratische Verkenningen* (2004) 111-121.
- C. van der Eijk and M.N. Franklin, eds, *Choosing Europe? The European Electorate and National Politics in the face of the Union* (Ann Arbor 1996).
- B.J.S. Hoetjes, 'The Parliament of the Netherlands and the European Union: Early Starter, Slow Mover', in: A. Maurer and W. Wessels, eds, *National Parliaments on their Ways to Europe: Losers or Latecomers?* (Baden-Baden 2001).
- B.J.S. Hoetjes, 'The Netherlands', in D. Rometsch and W. Wessels, eds., *The European Union and member states – towards institutional fusion?* (Manchester/New York 1996).
- R. Holzhacker, *The Power of Opposition Parties in National Parliaments to Scrutinize EU Decision-making in the Member States: Comparing Law, Institutions and Party Behaviours*, Conference paper, 21-22 May 2004, University of Limerick.
- J.I. Israel, *The Dutch republic. Its rise, greatness and fall* (Oxford 1995).
- J.J.H. Janssen, *Publieke steun voor de Europese Unie – analyse van de publieke opinie in 12 lidstaten 1952-1998* (Maastricht 2001).
- Ph. Kiiver, *The National Parliaments in the European Union – A Critical View on EU Constitution-Building* (The Hague/London/New York 2006).
- A. Lijphart, *Patterns of Democracy. Government Forms and Performance in Thirty-Six Countries* (London/New Haven 1999).
- N. MacCormick, 'The European Constitutional Process: A Theoretical View', in M.Escamilla and M.Saavedra, eds., *Anales de la catedra francisco suarez* (Plenary sessions of the Conference of the International Association for Philosophy of Law and Social Philosophy, May 2005, Granada).
- J.A. Peters, 'National Parliaments and Subsidiarity: Think Twice', 1 *European Constitutional Law Review* (2005) 68-72.
- C.W. van der Pot and A.M. Donner, *Handboek van het nederlandse staatsrecht* (Deventer, 2001).
- J.L. Price, *Holland and the Dutch republic in the seventeenth century. The politics of particularism* (Oxford 1994).
- H.H. Rowen and A. Lossky, eds., *Political ideas and institutions in the Dutch republic* (Los Angeles 1995).

- M.P.C.M. van Schendelen, 'The Netherlands: From Founding Father to Mounding Baby', in: Ph. Norton, ed., *National Parliaments and the European Union* (London/ New York 2004).
- S. Walgrave, T. Caals, M. Suetens and K. de Swert, *Ministerial cabinets and partitocracy. A career pattern study of ministerial cabinet members in Belgium* (2004/ 7) PSW Paper, University of Antwerp.

CHAPTER 7

The Croatian Parliament in Transition

From Authoritarian Past to European Future

Siniša Rodin

1 Introduction

Croatian parliamentary history reaches beyond the history of the modern Croatian state. The first documented session of the Croatian parliament and the first mention of its present name – Sabor – reaches back as far as to 1273. Following that year, the Croatian parliament existed in various forms and frameworks, such as under the Habsburg monarchy, the Kingdom of Yugoslavia under the dynasty of Karadordevic, or under the Communist rule of Josip Broz Tito. At the same time the Sabor transformed from a feudal representation of the nobility into a representative body of the people, although the inclusiveness of popular representation varied from period to period. The Sabor led Croatia's way out of feudalism in 1848, out of the Habsburg monarchy in 1918, out of fascism in 1944, out of centralised Communist power in 1974, and out of the Yugoslav Socialist federation in 1990. Now, for the first time in history, the Croatian democratic parliament has an opportunity to lead Croatia *into* something – the European Union.

It is not the purpose of this contribution to explore the history of the Croatian parliament, nor to evaluate its role in the creation of the Croatian state. Nor it is my intention to discuss the general constitutional setting in which the Croatian parliament operates today. My intention is rather limited to an attempt to show that regardless of the democratic transition facilitated by the adoption of Croatia's first-ever democratic constitution on the eve of 1991,[1] some of Croatian parliamentary practices still carry the baggage of the authoritarian past, and that the said baggage is loaded not primarily in the constitutional framework as developed after 1990, but in Croatian legal and political culture, understood as the system of shared beliefs, values, customs, behaviours, and artifacts that the members of society use in order to cope with their world and with one another, and that are transmitted from generation to generation through learning.[2] Within this limited objective I will focus on two parliamentary practices that have crystallised from the 1990s onwards, namely, the practice of so-called authentic interpretation of laws, and the practice of stringent control of governmental action, especially in the domain of external relations. Both practices, I submit, can be explained by a number of factors, such as an insufficient legislative framework, post-communist inertia, and selective perception of key political actors, or a specific political landscape. As such practices are significantly impairing the ability of Croatia to integrate into decision-making structures of the European Union, they will, arguably, have to be changed before accession.

1 The first-ever democratic constitution of Croatia was adopted on 22 December 1990. See e.g. Šarin (1997). The constitution was drafted by a committee composed of 229 members.

2 Bates (2005).

2 Enforcing Interpretative Supremacy

The powers of the Croatian parliament are defined by the constitution and by the parliamentary rules of procedure. Although, in the words of the first President of the Republic '...the Constitution makes the final departure from the system of communist, so-called socialist-self-management, based on social ownership...',[3] the constitution was, in fact, adopted pursuant to the constitution of Socialist Croatia of 1974. Following the free elections held in May 1990, the old constitutional structure4 was accommodated to the democratic principle. In constitutional terms, Croatia's institutional transition to independence was evolutionary rather than revolutionary. In the following years, Croatia went through a number of constitutional amendments that gradually changed the model of governance from a French-modelled semi-presidential to a parliamentary system, and from a bicameral to a unicameral structure.[5] The mentioned changes, introduced in late 2000 and early 2001, respectively, represent a major shift in the Croatian constitutional structure since independence. Above all, they signalled a possible revival of the traditionally dominant place that the parliament had in Croatian history. Though often suppressed, the perception of the parliament 'above which there is only God'[6] started to re-emerge in the minds of the political class. The practice of so-called *authentic interpretation* emerged in the same political context.

The power of the parliament to interpret laws is based on its rules of procedure[7] and is accepted by the constitutional court.[8] According to Articles 172 and 173 of the rules of procedure, the power to pass interpretation is vested in the parliamentary committee for legislation acting subject to a proposal from the government, and after having obtained a prior opinion of the parliamentary committee that had originally introduced the bill. The committee for legislation

3 *Vjesnik*, 22 December 2005.

4 Under the 1974 constitution, the Croatian parliament comprised three houses: the house of municipalities, the socio-political house and the house of associated labour.

5 The consolidated constitutional text is published in *Narodne novine* No. 41/2001 of 7 May 2001. Earlier publications and subsequent amendments include the *Ustav Republike Hrvatske, Narodne novine* 56/1990, the *Ustavni zakon o izmjenama i dopunama Ustava Republike Hrvatske, Narodne novine* 135/1997, *Promjena Ustava Republike Hrvatske, Narodne novine* 113/2000 and *Promjena Ustava Republike Hrvatske, Narodne novine* 28/2001.

6 This was first formulated as one of the political principles in 1861 by the 19th century politician Ante Starčević, in the context of the republican resistance to the Austro-Hungarian monarchy. Carl Schmitt (1988) noticed the perseverance of theological concepts in democratic societies: 'All significant concepts of the modern theory of the state are secularized theological concepts.'

7 *Poslovnik Hrvatskog sabora, Narodne novine* No. 9/2001.

8 See the decision of the constitutional court No. U-II-1265/2000, of 21 September 2004. According to the constitutional court, the power of the parliament to interpret laws is inherent to its general legislative powers.

formulates the final text of the interpretation and submits it to the parliament for adoption. It is to be published like any other piece of legislation, and courts apply it as an integral part of the act which it interprets.[9] So far the parliament passed 19 decisions on authentic interpretation,[10] six of those rejecting the interpretative bill.[11] The number of interpretations escalated after 1998.

The practice of authentic interpretation gradually evolved in two directions. On the one hand, it became widely accepted at the municipal[12] and administrative[13] level. On the other hand, the parliamentary committee for legislation started to issue interpretative 'comfort letters' to different constituencies, and such letters became generally understood as valid statements of law.[14] As far as the substance of such interpretative acts is concerned, they cover a wide range of legislative areas and, typically, have retroactive effects. They also affect cases pending before courts by changing the legal positions of parties.[15]

The practice of passing interpretative laws is not unknown to some other European legal systems, such as the Belgian, French, Greek, or Italian. However, there it is subject to a prohibition of retroactivity, and to a prohibition of interference with pending judicial disputes. These requirements are also

---

9 See e.g. the decision (*Rješenje*) of the supreme court, No. Rev-629/00-2. The supreme court applied authentic interpretation as an integral part of interpreted law with retroactive effect.

10 These decisions were published in *Narodne novine*: N.n. No. 91/1992; N.n. No. 175/2004; N.n. No. 28/1996; N.n. No. 58/2004; N.n. No. 3/94, 100/1996, 131/1997 and 129/2000; N.n. No. 101/2003; N.n. No. 78/2003; N.n. No. 33/2001; N.n. No. 60/2001; N.n. No. 48/1999; N.n. No. 127/2000; N.n. No. 119/2000; N.n. No. 109/2000; N.n. No.. 64/2000; N.n. 34/99; N.n. No. 121/1999; N.n. No. 96/1993 and 39/1995; N.n. No. 29/1999; N.n. No. 23/1999 and N.n. No. 25/1999; N.n. No. 21/1996.; N.n. No. 16/1998; N.n. No. 19/1990 and 19/1992; N.n. No. 34/1992.

11 Sometimes the parliament interprets a law by a decision rejecting the interpretative bill. In such cases it usually states that the law needs no authentic interpretation since it bears a clear meaning which is normally specified in such decisions. Such decisions are entitled 'Decision on not-giving an authentic interpretation.' See e.g. N.n. No. 167/2003; N.n. No. 33/2001 and 60/2001; N.n. No. 106/2003; N.n. No. 150/200; N.n. No. 22/2002; N.n. No. 22/2002.

12 The constitutional court is seemingly not prepared to allow the same power of authentic interpretation to municipal representative bodies as it allows to the parliament. See Odluka Ustavnog suda br. U-II-1362/2005U-VIII-3569/2005 of 12 October 2005, *Narodne novine* 125/2005.

13 See e.g. Overview of interpretations of the joint committee for interpretation and monitoring of the implementation of the basic collective agreement for public servants (Pregled tumačenja zajedničke komisije za tumačenje i praćenje primjene temeljnog kolektivnog ugovora za službenike i namještenike u javnim službama, Zagreb, October 2004, Uduga poslodavaca u Zdravstvu, Zagreb, 2004).

14 Such comfort letters are issued by the parliamentary committee on legislation, or sometimes by its chairperson. They are sent out on the official letterhead of the committee. Reported by HINA news agency and Index.hr news service on 10 November 2005 at www.index.hr/clanak.aspx?id=291440.

15 See e.g. authentic interpretation of 26 March 1999, *Narodne novine* No. 29/99, in which the parliament 'interpreted' the concept of 'honest possessor' and thereby changed the legal positions of certain possessors.

upheld by the European Court of Human Rights, as clarified in the leading *Stran Greek Refineries* case.[16]

Apart from being contrary to the European Convention on Human Rights, the Croatian art of authentic interpretation is problematic on at least two other counts. First, it diverts the interpretation of laws from the judicial to the legislative and administrative branch, restricts the parliamentary discourse on the meaning of rules, and substitutes the democratic process. Its further negative effects can be described as limiting interpretative autonomy of judges, and adversely affecting the self-awareness of the judiciary. Second, it is especially problematic in the light of Croatia's prospective membership of the European Union. On this count, problems can be identified in a semantic, normative and structural dimension.

In its *semantic* dimension, a problem emerges as to the meaning of rules of European Community law. According to Article 220 of the EC Treaty, '[t]he Court of Justice and the Court of First Instance, each within its jurisdiction, shall ensure that in the interpretation and application of this Treaty the law is observed.' One of the principal methods by which Community law is interpreted by the ECJ is preliminary rulings jurisdiction under Article 234 EC. The Croatian practice of authentic interpretation, as it stands today, opens the possibility of authentic interpretation of any legislation, including legislation implementing Community law, and that interpretation, and thus the meaning of the law, could, conceivably, be different from the interpretation given by the ECJ under its preliminary rulings jurisdiction.

In its *normative* dimension, authentic interpretation is limited by principles of supremacy and direct effect of Community law. As explained by the ECJ in *Costa*[17] and *Simmenthal*,[18] all national law, both substantive and procedural, that

16 *Stran Greek Refineries and Stratis Andreadis* v. *Greece*, ECtHR 22/1993/417/496; see also *Agoudimos and Cefallonian Sky Shipping Co.* v. *Greece*, ECtHR 38703/97, 28 June 2001: 'The Court reaffirms that while in principle the legislature is not precluded in civil matters from adopting new retrospective provisions to regulate rights arising under existing laws, the principle of the rule of law and the notion of fair trial enshrined in Article 6 preclude any interference by the legislature – other than on compelling grounds of the general interest – with the administration of justice designed to influence the judicial determination of a dispute'; *Zielinski and Pradal and Gonzalez and Others* v. *France*, ECtHR 24846/94 and 34165/96 to 34173/96, 28 October 1999; *Papageorgiou v. Greece*, ECtHR 97/1996/716/913, 22 October 1997.

17 Case 6/64, *Costa* v. *E.N.E.L.*, [1964] ECR 585: 'The law stemming from the Treaty, an independent source of law, could not because of its special and original nature, be overridden by domestic legal provisions, however framed, without being deprived of its character as Community law and without the legal basis of the community itself being called into question'.

18 Case 106/77, *Amministrazione delle Finanze dello Stato* v. *Simmenthal SpA*, [1978] ECR 629, at pt. 22: 'Accordingly, any provision of a national legal system and any legislative, administrative or judicial practice which might impair the effectiveness of Community law by withholding from the national court having jurisdiction to apply such law the power to do everything necessary at the moment of its application to set aside national legislative provisions which might prevent community rules from having full force and effect are incompatible with those requirements which are the very essence of Community law'.

stands in the way of the application of Community law, has to be set aside by national courts, and according to the ECJ, the validity of Community law cannot be affected by allegations that it runs counter to principles of national constitutional practice.[19] In other words, it is the normative demand of Community law that rules of Community law have immunity from authentic interpretation.

This brings us to the *structural* dimension of the problem where interpretative jurisdiction of the ECJ and of the Croatian parliament would collide. In the area of the application of Community law, the ECJ holds a firm position about its interpretative supremacy. Any claim as to authentic interpretation would create a conflict with the attitude[20] and the standing practice[21] of the ECJ.

3 Establishing Control over the Executive

Although parliamentary supremacy is nothing unusual in parliamentary practice in Europe, at least since the English Glorious Revolution of 1688, the question regarding the proper allocation of external relations powers between the legislative and the executive branch remains an issue in many jurisdictions. The issue that I will focus on concerns the insistence of the Croatian parliament to control the government in the exercise of its external relations powers. While parliamentary supremacy does not in any respect adversely affect Croatia's envisaged membership of the EU, the proper allocation of powers may significantly influence the efficiency of the fulfilment of Croatia's commitments and obligations. In that respect I maintain that the Croatian executive needs more explicitly defined constitutional authority in European affairs, whether when acting within the Stabilisation and Association Council[22] or within the Council of Ministers. At the same time, the Croatian parliament will need broader and more efficient supervisory powers, and a more clearly defined role in supranational decision-making.

As Croatian law stands today, the role of the parliament in external relations is limited. The parliament has to ratify treaties that require legislative enactment, treaties of 'military' and 'political' nature, and treaties implying financial

---

[19] Case 11/70, *Internationale Handelsgesellschaft mbH* v. *Einfuhr- und Vorratsstelle für Getreide und Futtermittel*, [1970] ECR 1125.

[20] Opinion 2/94 of 28 March 1996, Accession by the Community to the European Convention for the Protection of Human Rights and Fundamental Freedoms, [1996] ECR I-1759.

[21] Case 11/70, footnote 19 *supra*.

[22] The Stabilisation and Association Council is established pursuant to Article 110 of the Stabilisation and Association Agreement. Under Article 111 thereof, it 'shall consist of the members of the Council of the European Union and members of the Commission of the European Communities, on the one hand, and of members of the Government of Croatia, on the other', OJ C 332 E/31.

obligations.[23] International treaties that have the effect of delegating constitutional powers to an international organisation or alliance have to be ratified by a two-thirds majority. Finally, treaties that lead to an association of Croatia into alliances with other states are subject to a specific procedure set by Article 141 of the constitution.[24] The mentioned provisions do not envisage any role of the parliament in external relations prior to the stage of ratification. Supervision of the government is possible through regular mechanisms of parliamentary control, such as parliamentary questions, interpellation or debate in the parliamentary committee for international relations, which discusses ratification bills. All these instruments have, however, limited effects.

On the other hand, direct constitutional authority for governmental action in the implementation of international treaties is also limited. Under Article 112 (4) of the Croatian constitution, the government is authorised to pass sub-regulations in order to implement 'laws', this expression being widely understood as *Gesetz* or *Loi*, i.e. acts of parliament. Although international treaties under Article 140 of the constitution form part of the national legal order and have legal force superior to laws, the government does not exercise its Article 112 (4) power to implement non-self-executing treaties. Apart from that, the government can also exercise delegated powers under Article 87 of the constitution. Subject to that Article, the parliament can authorise the government to pass regulations during a one-year term and subject to subsequent parliamentary ratification. The same article defines the exclusive regulatory powers of the parliament (German: *Gesetzesvorbehalt*). Those are regulations concerning constitutional rights and liberties, ethnic rights, the electoral system, the organisation, jurisdiction and methods of work of state authorities, and local self-government. Thus, they cannot be delegated to the government. The practice of extending the authority for delegated regulation in matters of internal policy has however been very generous. Laws delegating regulatory authority use broad language such as 'regulation of commerce'. In the light of such generous delegation, the constitutional court has warned the parliament to be more specific when delegating regulatory powers to the government.[25]

While the Croatian parliament is generally unspecific about the delegation of internal powers to the government, this is different in external relations. Briefly put, there is a relatively widespread understanding among Croatian political parties that the government should be under strict parliamentary supervision

---

[23] Article 139 of the constitution. To the same effect see also Article 18 of the law on the making and implementation of international treaties (Zakon o sklapanju i izvršavanju međunarodnih ugovora), N.n. 28/1996.

[24] That Article requires a two-thirds parliamentary majority and a national referendum.

[25] Decision of the constitutional court U-II-66/1994 of 25 February 1994, *Narodne novine* No. 16/1994; see also Crnić (1994) 20. The Croatian constitution does not entail any provisions that would restrict a delegation of powers, such as e.g. Article 80 of the German Grundgesetz which makes delegation subject to a strict definition of its contents, purpose and scope.

when external or European policy is at stake. The latter attitude was exemplified in political practice in several instances. One of the most significant attempts of the parliament to control governmental action in European affairs is related to the implementation of the Stabilisation and Association Agreement (SAA) with the EU.[26]

During the ratification of the SAA, the issue emerged whether regulatory powers have to be transferred to the Stabilisation and Association Council – a decision-making body envisaged by Article 112 of the SAA. Due to the political balance in the Croatian parliament, the Agreement was ratified by a majority of all representatives, yet falling short of the two-thirds majority which is required for a transfer of powers.[27] In response to the right-wing parties claiming that the SAA is stripping Croatia of her national sovereignty, the Croatian prime-minister and the minister for European integration assessed the SAA as an ordinary international law treaty, and did not push for a two-thirds majority ratification which would have been required by the constitution in case of a delegation of regulatory powers to supranational bodies.[28] This method of ratification gave rise to questions whether the Stabilisation and Association Council would have law-making authority, and if so, whether its decisions could create individual rights in the Croatian legal order. The Croatian parliament subsequently adopted a law implementing the Stabilisation and Association Agreement,[29] apparently in line with the position that the Stabilisation and Association Council may not, without further implementing measures, exercise constitutional regulatory powers. Accordingly, as Croatian law stands today, law made under the SAA cannot have direct effect in the Croatian legal order. Article 6 of the mentioned law applies a radical dualist approach according to which decisions of the Association Council are subject to parliamentary ratification. This is a clear departure from the constitutional mandate of monism stipulated under Article 140 of the constitution, which renders ratified international treaties part of national law. For that reason, compatibility of the SAA implementation law with the constitution is questionable.

By limiting the regulatory powers of the Stabilisation and Association Council, the parliament also restricted the government's autonomy to participate in making secondary legislation subject to the SAA. In this way the parliament limited the shift of power from the legislative to the executive branch, which is a well-known phenomenon both in EU member states and candidate coun-

---

26 Stabilisation and Association Agreement between the European Communities and their Member States, of the one part, and the Republic of Croatia, of the other part, OJ L26, 28 January 2005, p. 1.

27 *Izvješća Hrvatskog Sabora* (Croatian Parliament's Reports), No. 315, 20 December 2001.

28 See e.g. the speech by minister Neven Mimica held before the Croatian parliament on 24 October 2001, saying that no constitutional regulatory authority will be delegated to the Stabilisation and Association Council, see www.mei.hr.

29 Zakon o provedbi sporazuma o stabilizaciji i pridruživanju, *Narodne novine*, Međunarodni ugovori (Official Gazette, International Treaties), No. 15/2001.

tries.[30] However, what is quite remarkable in the Croatian case, is an attempt of the parliament to subject the application of legal sources under the SAA to more stringent requirements than is the case with sources of other international treaties. The more precise an obligation, the more stringent the parliamentary control.

Another attempt to limit the playground of the executive in European affairs came from the Croatian Peasants' Party, which on 15 March 2004 instituted an interpellation concerning negotiations on protocol 7 to the SAA.[31] The main claim on which the interpellation was based was excess of powers of the executive, i.e. an objection that the government was negotiating the protocol without having obtained the consent of the parliament, even though such a consent is not required under Croatian law.[32] Insistence on parliamentary approval in the stage of negotiations is an indicator of the understanding that the government's position to the parliament is subordinate, even in cases where the government is acting pursuant to an explicit legal basis. Namely, subject to article 112 of the constitution, the government has the authority to pursue external policy. This is to be exercised within the limits set by the parliament, but it does not imply an obligation to consult the parliament every time an external policy action is taken. So far the Croatian parliament has expressed its European policy views on many occasions, just to mention the resolution on accession of Croatia to the European Union of 18 December 2002, the national programme for accession to the EU, or the application for membership of the EU submitted to the Greek EU presidency on 21 February 2003. These, as well as other political instruments, are providing for the political framework within which the government can exercise its constitutional authority without day-to-day parliamentary supervision. In any case, the new position of the government in the European decision-making process, as well as the need for passing implementing legislation to give full effect to European secondary law, calls for a rethinking of the present constitutional framework.

While the supervisory role of the parliament in European affairs is not questioned, and its participatory role has to be enforced,[33] it is also desirable to estab-

30 See Sadurski (2004).

31 Protocol to the Stabilisation and Association Agreement between the European Communities and their Member States, of the one part, and the Republic of Croatia, of the other part, to take account of the accession of the Czech Republic, the Republic of Estonia, the Republic of Cyprus, the Republic of Hungary, the Republic of Latvia, the Republic of Lithuania, the Republic of Malta, the Republic of Poland, the Republic of Slovenia and the Slovak Republic to the European Union, OJ L26, 28 January 2005, p. 222.

32 Law on the making and implementation of international treaties (Zakon o sklapanju i izvršavanju međunarodnih ugovora), N.n. No. 28/1996.

33 See e.g. Protocol on the role of national parliaments in the European Union, OJ C310/204 of 16 December 2004, providing for '... greater involvement of national Parliaments in the activities of the European Union and to enhance their ability to express their views on draft European legislative acts as well as on other matters...'.

lish a direct constitutional authority that would provide the government with a constitutional basis for making decisions in European institutions, and for implementing them into national law, where required by Community law. This would preferably be accompanied by a simultaneous obligation to inform the parliament regularly about forthcoming regulatory activities. Also, as decisions of the government, when it exercises delegated powers, are subject to a parliamentary mandate and subsequent approval, the discretion of the government in European affairs will strongly depend on the parliamentary definition of the mandate, and the parliament's readiness to approve the measures adopted by the government. This can potentially make the government's role in implementing Community law more difficult.

Generally speaking, at present, the Croatian parliament leaves the government more discretion to pursue national policy, whereas it exercises stricter supervision in external affairs. As government involvement in European affairs becomes more frequent and substantial, turning European and formerly external affairs into domestic ones, the need for a re-definition of parliamentary supervision will become more pressing. As the involvement of national parliaments in EU affairs is a matter for every member state to decide on its own, and approaches in member states differ, Croatia is in need of opening a public debate on this issue, within the framework of the constitutional adjustment for EU membership.

4 Explaining the Parliament's Vigilance

Examples of authentic interpretation of laws, and scrutiny of the government's action in European affairs, indicate the vigilant stance of the Croatian parliament in the exercise of some of its alleged powers. As we have seen, the parliament has shown its intention to control the interpretation and application of the law in the grey zones of the constitutional separation of powers.[34] While this creeping supremacy may seem to be a predictable consequence of institutional logic, there are some other possible explanations of the described process, notably: a normative deficit (section 4.1 below), post-communist inertia / selective perception (4.2) and the political landscape (4.3).

4.1 Normative Deficit

First, by asserting its powers, the parliament is substituting normative deficits at the constitutional and legislative level, where the existing constitutional and legislative framework for both the allocation of external powers between the three branches of government, as well as for the interpretation of laws, is insufficient.

34 Constitution, Article 4.

The parliamentary role in external relations is limited, and the parliament has a voice only in the ratification procedure. In the absence of communication with the government during treaty negotiations, there is a risk of international treaties being negotiated and signed by the government without a permissive political consensus. This has occurred in at least two instances: in July 2001, the parliament of Croatia has declined to ratify an already initialled draft border treaty with Slovenia that was due to solve the border issue between the two states.[35] In the absence of parliamentary approval, the treaty was not signed. Similarly, a draft treaty on restitution of property with Austria was initialled on 4 April 2005, but not signed due to heavy parliamentary opposition.[36]

As far as European affairs are concerned, the situation started to change in the second half of 2005, on the eve of negotiations for membership with the EU. The normative deficit was addressed by the Croatian parliament by adopting three instruments: a resolution on strategic positions for negotiations with the EU, a declaration of the parliament on fundamental principles of negotiations for membership of the EU, and a common statement of the parliament and the government on joint action in the process of negotiations for membership of the EU.[37] The mentioned instruments provided for modalities of co-operation between the government and the parliament via the establishment of a national committee for monitoring negotiations. The committee comprises 15 members of the parliament, six of whom, as well as the chairman, are drawn from the parliamentary opposition; four members are external and are appointed by the President of the Republic, the academic community, employers' associations and unions, respectively. The committee can discuss negotiating positions and give recommendations to the government. The government has to report on the progress in negotiations at least once every three months. This arrangement clearly demonstrates the need to provide for permissive political consensus in advance of undertaking international commitments. It is a welcome innovation that might minimise the need for informal political pressure on the government in the process of negotiations, and channel political debate. However, it is highly desirable to transform the emerging political practice into legislative instruments that would serve not only the purpose of treaty negotiations, but possibly the decision-making process at European level once the time comes.

The practice of authentic interpretation of laws can be also explained, at least in part, by the parliament's wish to remedy a normative deficit. Due to histori-

---

35 See e.g. Branko Podgornik in *Novi list*, 25 September 2001.

36 See information of the ministry of justice at www.pravosudje.hr/default.asp?ru=1&gl=200511290000001&sid=&jezik=1.

37 Rezolucija o strategijskim odrednicama pregovora Republike Hrvatske s Europskom unijom, N.n. No. 122/2005; Deklaracija Hrvatskoga sabora o temeljnim načelima pregovora za punopravno članstvo Republike Hrvatske u Europskoj uniji, N.n. No. 12/2005; Izjava Hrvatskoga sabora i Vlade Republike Hrvatske o zajedničkom djelovanju u procesu pregovora za članstvo u Europskoj uniji, N.n. 12/2005.

cal and doctrinal reasons, Croatian courts interpret laws strictly. Interpretative autonomy of judges is not appreciated, and law is taken to have an objective meaning that cannot be changed by interpretation. Legal reasoning is deductive, based on definitions that often do not correspond to reality but are transmitted from the top to the lower levels of the judicial hierarchy. As the function of adjudication is understood as 'applying the law', and not as solving disputes between parties, possible lacunae are often not filled by judicial interpretation, but by recourse to the parliament.

4.2 Post-Communist Inertia / Selective Perception

I am using term post-communist inertia to describe a situation in which different concepts or practices of socialist law are disassociated from their ideological contents and applied within the democratic constitutional framework. Examples of such concepts or practices are, for example, the understanding of the constitution as a political, rather than legal instrument, a top-down instead of bottom-up approach to the political process or to legal interpretation and, certainly, the understanding of the role of the executive and the judiciary in terms of unity instead of separation of powers, both branches being subservient to the legislature – once the people's assembly, today the parliament.[38] Both parliamentary practices discussed in this contribution can be explained by post-communist inertia, as they both result from a perpetuation of the concept of unity of power. Seen in this light, authentic interpretation of laws and strict parliamentary control of the government in external relations are just different instances of failure to fully implement the constitutional principle of separation of powers.[39] They originate from the same conceptual background according to which, for example, emperor Justinian threatened interpreting the *Corpus Iuris Civilis* with capital punishment,[40] or according to which the constitution of the Soviet Union of 1936 vested *ius interpretandi* in the presidium of the Supreme Soviet.[41]

---

38 For these and other instances of post-communist inertia see Rodin (2005).

39 Another example is the perpetuation of a dualist approach to international law, despite the constitutional mandate of monism. See e.g. Rodin (2003).

40 According to the maxim *'eius est interpretari leges, cuius est condere'*, see Schott (2002).

41 Article 121 of the constitution of the USSR (1936). Authentic interpretation probably originates from Justinian, see Moyle (1912); it can also be found in other legal systems, e.g. canonic law. In the law of contemporary democracies (e.g. Italy and Belgium) authentic interpretation is restricted by a prohibition of retroactivity, a prohibition of interference with adjudication and pending proceedings. On the other hand, it is not present in Germany, or the United States. For the US, see e.g. Holmes (1898-1899) 420: 'In this country, at least, for constitutional reasons, if for no other, if the same legislature that passed it should declare at a later date a statute to have a meaning which in the opinion of the court the words did not bear, I suppose that the declaratory act would have no effect upon intervening transactions unless in a place and case where retrospective legislation was allowed.'

Having said this, I do not want to suggest that Croatian parliamentarians, civil servants or judges are deliberately following some hidden nostalgic agendas. My claim is rather based on the theory of perception originally presented by Bruner and Postman in 1949.[42] The basic axioms of the theory are that perceiving is a process '...which results from the stimulation of a prepared or *eingestellt* organism' and that perceptions are organised in such way '...as to maximize percepts relevant to current needs and expectations and to minimize percepts inimical to such needs and expectations.' The theory is based on an experiment in which subjects were shown a pack of playing cards and were asked to distinguish between normal and 'trick' cards, such as a red king of spades. The experiment showed that, instead of reality, subjects selectively perceived what they expected to see. Other experiments showed that personal values play a significant role in the learning process. 'Since individuals tend to perceive selectively in accordance with their basic values, or interests, it seems reasonable to suppose that they will also acquire new perceptual habits in a manner consistent with their particular value orientation.'[43] In other words, individuals incline to see what is familiar to them, and to suppress unfamiliar things as irrelevant. For the purposes of the present discussion, de-ideologisised legal and political concepts are perceived, while the new democratic constitutional framework is suppressed. New legal and political concepts, such as separation of powers or interpretative autonomy of the judiciary, being imported instead of developed, are being suppressed as irrelevant by key political actors. Therefore authentic interpretation, therefore the subservience of the government.

4.3 The Political Landscape

More intensive parliamentary involvement in the government's day-to-day affairs may also be explained by the specific political structure following the parliamentary elections of 3 January 2000 and 3 December 2003.

The political coalition that won a mandate to form the government in 2000 comprised six parliamentary political parties led by the Social-Democratic Party. The politically heterogeneous coalition was driven by a common goal: to democratise the political system, and to introduce constitutional changes that would dismantle presidential governance. In circumstances where not every coalition party was participating in the government to the same extent, coalition partners started to exercise more stringent parliamentary control of the executive. It was exactly in the period following the parliamentary elections of 2000 when the contentious law implementing the Stabilisation and Association Agreement was adopted, and the number of authentic interpretations started

---

42 Bruner and Postman (1949-1950).

43 Bruner and Goodman (1947) understand perceptual fixation as being characterised by *selection, accentuation* and *fixation*, processes which ultimately lead to the 'persistence and preferential retention of certain selected precepts.'

to escalate.[44] The relatively weak political position of the government continued following the elections of 2003. The government led by the Croatian Democratic Union was formed almost as a minority government, only with the support of representatives of national minorities and the small Croatian Pensioners' Party. The described political landscape provided for a fertile ground for frequent opposition, such as the described interpellation of 25 March 2004, but it was not limited to the area of external relations.

The precarious position of the government is amplified by the legislative procedure envisaged for passing organic laws under article 82 of the Croatian constitution. Subject to that provision, laws regulating rights of national minorities have to be passed by a two-thirds majority, while several other areas of regulation, including human rights and freedoms, have to be passed by a majority of all votes.[45] A stricter majority is also required for the ratification of international treaties delegating constitutional powers and, by implication, treaties regulating human rights. In the absence of meaningful consultation procedures prior to ratification, parliamentary parties can only have recourse to regular instruments of parliamentary supervision, such as interpellations, specific restrictive laws, or soft-law instruments.[46] In brief, the political heterogeneity of government coalitions, the particularly uneven representation and voice of coalition partners at governmental level, as well as the weak political position of the two recent governments, have undoubtedly contributed to the enhanced parliamentary control of the government's work.

5 Conclusion

The Croatian constitution is a democratic one, providing for parliamentary democracy, separation of powers, government limited by law, and protection of human rights and freedoms, including the rights of minorities. These constitutional choices are supported by democratic institutions, and guaranteed by political and legal procedures. However, an insufficient normative framework accompanied by selective perception on the side of key political actors, and specific political circumstances, have contributed to the perpetuation of certain parliamentary practices that have their origin in the pre-democratic political order. Both authentic interpretation of laws and parliamentary super-

---

44 On 5 December 2001, see footnote 29 *supra*.

45 The constitutional court is interpreting the notion of human rights legislation broadly, see e.g. a recent decision setting aside the public assembly act, due to an insufficient number of votes. Decision of the constitutional court U-I-3307/2005 of 23 November 2005. See also decision U-I-2566/2003, U-I-2892/2003 of 27 November 2003 setting aside the criminal code amendment act for the same reason. In both decisions the constitutional court held that the contested legislation regulated human rights based on an insufficient parliamentary majority.

46 See footnote 37 *supra*.

vision of the executive are of course also exercised in other democratic states. However, the parliamentary interpretation of laws is always subject to a prohibition of retroactivity and a condition of non-interference with pending judicial cases, while scrutiny of the government is driven by interests of democratic pluralist control, and the constitutional principle of checks and balances, rather than by an understanding of the government as an executive committee of the assembly. As far as Croatia is concerned, in both areas there is a need for change of the legislative framework. Authentic interpretation can easily be dismantled by changing the parliamentary rules of procedure. Nevertheless, the change will have to be facilitated by changing legal and political culture as well. That would imply courts taking the responsibility for legal interpretation, instead of relying on ready-made legislative precepts. In that way the meaning of law will gradually start being developed in an inter-institutional and social dialogue, instead of being defined and communicated downwards from the top.

As far as the government's powers in European and, more generally, external affairs are concerned, Croatia's membership of the EU calls for substantial constitutional amendments. In the political sphere, the government needs more autonomy in negotiating national positions in European institutions, while in the legal sphere acts adopted at European level in which the government is participating have to be availed direct effect without further parliamentary action. Also, the government will need an explicit constitutional authority for passing regulations for the implementation of non-self-executing European acts. At the same time, the parliament needs a voice in the formulation of European policies, as well as procedures for the exercise of subsidiarity competencies. Also, the Croatian constitution will have to find a solution for a constructive, co-operative, pluralist and transparent relationship between the parliament and the government in European law and policy-making. Although the mentioned changes are certainly needed for Croatia's EU membership, they would in fact be highly desirable as soon as possible, bearing in mind Croatia's commitments under the Stabilisation and Association Agreement.

The described parliamentary practices developed as a result of a number of historical, psychological and practical factors. It will not be possible to change them by legislation only. As we have seen, harmonisation of law does not necessarily entail semantic harmonisation. Newly introduced democratic institutions and laws have first to be perceived by the relevant audience in order to be incorporated into day-to-day practices. In other words, institutions and laws need not only to be formally harmonised to apparently resemble their European model. They have to be *selected, accentuated,* and *fixed* in the minds of key social players. They need to bear the meaning assigned to them within the framework of the democratic and pluralist paradigm. That goal cannot be achieved by vertical measures, such as legislation, only. What is needed is an implementation of horizontal measures, such as education, discussion, and communication. At the same time, any political or legal practices suppressing transparency, participation and democratic pluralist control will not stand up to scrutiny either.

References

- D.G. Bates, *Human Adaptive Strategies: Culture, Ecology, and Politics*, 3rd ed. (Boston 2005).
- J.S. Bruner and C. Goodman, 'Values and need as organizing factors in perception', 47 *J. abnorm. soc. Psychol.* (1947) 33-44.
- J.S. Bruner and L. Postman, 'On the Perception of Incongruity: A Paradigm', 18 *Journal of Personality* (1949-1950) 206-223.
- J. Crnić, *Vladavina Ustava* (Zagreb 1994).
- O. W. Holmes, 'Theory of Interpretation', 12 *Harv. L. Rev.* (1898-1899).
- J.B. Moyle, *Comp. Imperatoris Iustiniani Institutionum, Introduction*, 5th ed. (Oxford 1912).
- S. Rodin, 'Discourse and Authority in European and Post-Communist Legal Culture', 1 *Croatian Yearbook of European Law and Policy* (2005) 1-22.
- S. Rodin, 'Stabilization and Association Agreement – A Hostage of Dualist Inertia', in Th. Bruha, B. Vrček and A. Graf Wass von Czege, eds, *Croatia on the Path to the EU: Political, Legal and Economic Aspects* (Hamburg 2003).
- W. Sadurski, 'Accession's Democracy Dividend: The Impact of the EU Enlargement upon Democracy in New Member States of Central and Eastern Europe', 10 *European Law Journal* (2004) 371-401.
- D. Šarin, 'Nastanak hrvatskog ustava', *Narodne Novine* 1997.
- C. Schott, 'Legal Culture – Report on the 34th Conference of German Legal Historians in Würzburg, 8-12 September 2002', 4 *German Law Journal* (2003).
- C. Schmitt, *Political Theology* (Cambridge, Mass. 1988).

CHAPTER 8

National Parliaments in the EU's Composite Constitution

A Plea for a Shift in Paradigm

Leonard F.M. Besselink

1 Introduction

In this essay I explore the meaning and implications of two paradigms for the role which national parliaments can play within the European Union's constitutional order. The first paradigm conceives of the EU's constitutional order in terms of 'levels'. Hence, I shall call this paradigm the 'multi-level paradigm' or simply 'levels paradigm'. The second is a paradigm which I shall call 'polycentric'. I first briefly elucidate the 'multilevel' paradigm and how it fits in with the present view of the role of national parliaments with regard to EU decision-making. Next I indicate how a more polycentric conception of the composite European constitutional order would view the role of national parliaments. I trace some signs of such a polycentric approach in the Treaty establishing a Constitution for Europe, and briefly hypothesise how such a polycentric view might offer better chances for the EU's opening up to accountability. In the next two sections I discuss the possibilities of a shift towards the latter paradigm without the Constitutional Treaty being adopted, and the research agenda that such a shift would imply.

2 'Paradigms'

Talking of paradigms is a manner of making explicit what otherwise remains more or less implicit in the manner of viewing reality. Paradigms concern the starting-points for looking at reality, they are a manner of speaking about perceived reality. They serve as explanatory devices for understanding reality and provide us with alternatives for perceiving reality.[1]

The discussion in this paper abstracts from much detail and nuance. This is partly because of lack of knowledge on the part of its author, and because of the size of this essay, but not just that. It is also linked to the distinction of 'paradigms' in the sense used here to abstract from some of the detail and nuance in the reality paradigms refer to. In this respect the paradigms I discuss are like 'models' in the Weberian sense of 'Idealmodelle' – but these lack the dynamic aspect inhering in the concept of paradigms as competing frames of reference for studying reality over time, during which these frames of reference may overlap, the one may dominate and another come to be superseded.

One further caveat immediately follows from this, and ought to precede our discussion of the substance. This essay is *not* aimed at analysing the scholarly literature and its paradigms; it does not have the aim of studying 'second order'

---

1 We do not need to agree on Thomas Kuhn's use of the concept and his analysis of shifts in paradigms as an explanation of scientific and scholarly development, as initially developed by Kuhn (1962), further refined in the postscript added to the second edition; nor do we have to agree with his critics. Here I submit that his conviction that the ideas he developed cannot be applied to the law (and legal studies) is to a large extent misplaced.

developments. Such an analysis could very well be undertaken, and perhaps it is a propitious moment to do so,[2] but the scope of the paper and the occasion of its writing makes this less opportune.

In this essay I will, then, take the two paradigms adumbrated to be manners of looking at one particular part of political reality, to wit, parliamentary practice with regard to European decision-making. In the course of doing so, I attempt to show that different manners of looking at reality ('paradigms') make a difference to finding ways of practical innovation, also in constitutional affairs.[3]

3 The Paradigm of the 'Multilevel' Constitution

The paradigm which conceives of the constitutional order of the EU and its member states as a construct comprising different 'levels', has been predominant. There are various forms which this paradigm has taken in the literature since the 1960s, the one more subtle than the other. I mention the recent coining of the expression 'multilevel constitutionalism' by Ingolf Pernice,[4] which on some points seems to develop a more sophisticated model than the classic European law approach which emerged in the 1960s and still dominates that discipline, but which on the whole ignored the relevance of national constitutional orders within the European construct by positing rather uncritically an unconditional primacy and predominance of EC (and even EU) law over whatever national constitutions might mean to or wish to say on European integration. What the various views hold in common, however, is the essential distinction of different 'levels'.

This thinking in terms of 'levels' has two implications. Firstly, the metaphor of 'levels' easily spills over into speaking of higher and lower levels. The paradigm thus reveals itself as being essentially hierarchical. Secondly, the idea of 'levels' suggests a relative separateness – a view which is compounded by an emphasis on the 'autonomy' claims for the relevant constitutional orders, particularly the EC order. In combining these two features, the paradigm suggests that the levels are in a sense separate from each other, but at the same time – viewed from a 'dynamic' perspective – it essentially leads to a situation

[2] In the Netherlands, there is a sudden wave of academic opinion which holds that the academic study of law has no method, and a sense of shame for it. Fortunately, this opinion is false, and the sense of shame entirely misplaced. To the extent that there is no single established scholarly method, the situation corresponds with Paul Feyerabend's ideal situation for meaningful science and progress; see Feyerabend (1975).

[3] This is so because, as G.B. Vico pointed out, human and therefore political reality is a man-made, or, more precisely, language-made reality. 'First order' discourse which constitutes practical reality, and 'second order' discourse reflecting on first order realities, are therefore intricately meshed in thee *scienza* with which we are dealing.

[4] See Pernice (1999) and Pernice (2002).

in which one level must outweigh or even supersede the other. The 'centre of gravity' within the system can only exist at one level at a time – the levels cannot be coextensive.[5]

The prevalence of the multilevel approach becomes evident when we look at the most common analysis of EU decision-making and the role of national parliaments. The prevailing doctrine of the democratic deficit hinges critically on the 'transfer' of powers from one 'level', the national 'level', to another: the European 'level'. Inherent in speaking of 'transfer', instead of, for instance, 'attribution' or, more neutrally, 'conferral' of powers, is the idea that once a previously national power has moved to the European level, it has somehow 'disappeared' at the national level. Indeed, as regards the decisional institutions, this has had as a consequence that national governments meeting through their representatives in the Council have become pivotal actors to the detriment of national parliaments, also with regard to matters which were previously – i.e. before the transfer to the European level – within the remit of national parliaments, notably legislative power. Not the parliament in the national capital, but Brussels decides.

The scrutiny of European decision-making by national parliaments, in the manner in which it has developed over time, may be thought to counteract this. But actually practice reinforces this way of viewing things. At the national level, governments are scrutinised as to the position which their national representative is to take, or has taken, in the Council in Brussels. Scrutiny thus becomes a purely national matter, aimed at national actors. Its meaning and importance is restricted to the national level. It is a matter of each individual capital. On the whole, the effect of this purely national scrutiny moves national parliaments into a 'monist' position towards their respective governments, in that the separateness of the roles of government and parliament within a national constitutional system is reduced. Scrutiny, which is on the whole distinctly non-partisan and almost a-political, is about articulating the *national* point of view of the member state to be represented in the Council, not about any particular *political* view to be represented at the EU level.

Governments may not like parliamentary scrutiny of what they intend to do in Brussels, particularly when such scrutiny is critical and acquires a certain intensity, but they know that they can also use it to bolster the national viewpoint in the Council.[6] So while it is not in the nature of governments of member

---

5 The more sophisticated recent literature acknowledges that there may be a kind of sequence of moments which makes 'shifts' possible from one level to another, which may even be caused by the 'interaction' between the levels. This brings this model close to the polycentric paradigm that I discuss below. I submit that some recent versions of the multilevel paradigm are at a breaking point from the classic one, which crucially hinges on the perception of 'levels' as mutually autonomous higher and lower levels. 'Multilevel' then becomes a misnomer for the actual theory propounded.

6 Contrary to what is often thought, there is no obligation in law for the *Danish* government which would tie it to the parliamentary mandate that it always seeks in the European affairs committee of the *Folket-*

states to ask for more intense parliamentary scrutiny of their behaviour, government representatives can be expected also to be able to play the card of national parliamentary problems with intended European decisions in Brussels which, if the game is played skilfully, strengthens their position in the Council. These monist tendencies resulting from parliamentary scrutiny may also explain why the French government at the time of the Maastricht Treaty found it politically acceptable to make a major change to the governmental system, and allow parliamentary resolutions to be directed to the government in European affairs,[7] whereas previously this was constitutionally forbidden as an encroachment on government prerogatives:[8] having a stronger parliament expressing itself on issues arising in Brussels might reinforce the French position in the EU.

So parliamentary scrutiny tends to reinforce a government's view as a solidified national point of view. Also, a national parliament's objections to a draft decision can politically be translated into a firmer position of the member state in the Council. Parliamentary scrutiny practiced in this form contributes to EU decision-making being conducted along predominantly national lines, rather than in a politically partisan manner cutting across internal European borders. This is so with decision-making at the EU level in the Council, and this is so in the parliamentary scrutiny procedures at the national level: European issues are rarely considered the object of partisan politics, but usually as non-partisan national politics. The game is one that is played at neatly compartmentalised 'levels'. It follows the rules and uses the vocabulary of the 'levels paradigm'.

---

ing; yet two governments fell over decisions they had agreed to in the Council in Brussels. There are commitments for the *French* government to seek parliament's views on draft decisions under Article 88-4 of the constitution, on the basis of a 'circulaire du premier ministre, en date du 19 juillet 1994'. Also, there exist similar obligations for the *British* government under a resolution which was first passed in 1980, *House of Commons Journals* 1979-1980, p. 819, reconfirmed in a resolution of 24 October 1990, p. 646; it was last reformulated in a resolution of 17 November 1998, see *Hansard*, 17 November 1998, Col. 803-804; also regularly published in an appendix to the standing orders of the House of Commons. The *German* government is bound under Article 23 (3) of the *Grundgesetz*, whereas the *Dutch* government is dependent on parliamentary consent for binding Third Pillar decisions, on the basis of the acts of parliament approving the respective treaty amendments since Maastricht, but under no obligation whatsoever as concerns other binding decisions.

7 Article 88-4 of the French constitution: 'Le Gouvernement soumet à l'Assemblée nationale et au Sénat, dès leur transmission au Conseil de l'Union européenne, les projets ou propositions d'actes des Communautés européennes et de l'Union européenne comportant des dispositions de nature législative. Il peut également leur soumettre les autres projets ou propositions d'actes ainsi que tout document émanant d'une institution de l'Union européenne. Selon des modalités fixées par le règlement de chaque assemblée, des résolutions peuvent être votées, le cas échéant en dehors des sessions, sur les projets, propositions ou documents mentionnés à l'alinéa précédent.'

8 For the previous situation cf. Conseil constitutionnel, nos. 59-2 and 3 DC, 17, 18, 24 June 1959, *Recueil Conseil constitutionnel*, 58.

4 A 'Polycentric' Paradigm

The European Union can also be viewed other than in terms of separate 'levels' only. For this it is necessary to take the Union not as merely 'Brussels', with 'Brussels' being shorthand for Council and Commission. Nor should it be taken as 'Brussels and Strasbourg' to include the European Parliament as well, nor as any other shorthand for the institutions, organs and bodies of the EC and EU. The European Union can under an alternative paradigm be taken as comprising not only the European institutions, but the member states as well, as is done in normal, everyday speech: the twenty-five member states make up the European Union.

If we focus on the constitutional order of the European Union, this view implies that it comprises not only the constitutional law of the EC and EU treaties and of secondary law, but also the constitutional law of the member states. The EU constitutional order is in this view a more truly composite legal order than is the case in the 'multilevel' approach. In the composite constitutional legal order as viewed here, the situation is polycentric rather than hierarchic, both with regard to substantive constitutional norms,[9] and institutionally. And here the national parliaments come into the picture. National parliaments are not isolated at the national level within the national system, but must be considered part of the larger EU constitutional order. This should imply that they also have a role to play within the broader EU framework, a role which is not constrained to the *national* arena, but precisely is one to be played in the *European* arena.

5 Towards the Polycentric Paradigm

The Treaty establishing a Constitution for Europe provides some interesting clues for this broadening of the context in which national parliaments can act. I point out a few of them. A very general clue, when taken on its own, is Article I-5, concerning the duty of the Union to respect the member states' 'national identities inherent in their fundamental structures, political and constitutional'. In a number of respects, the meaning of this provision is not absolutely clear.[10] We cannot treat them all in the context of this essay. Here I merely point out that the provision may be understood in two ways, each of which corresponds to one of the two paradigms outlined above.

9 The protection of fundamental rights at EU level is a case in point.

10 Clearly, this Article must be read in the context of the counterbalancing Article I-6 on the EU law's 'primacy over the law of the member states'. This primacy need not be understood in a hierarchical sense, as is often done by European law specialists. At any rate, this Article I-6 in turn must be read without ignoring Article I-5. But there are many other questions of textual and contextual construction of Article I-5.

First, the provision can be read in accordance with the distinct 'levels' approach as meaning that the national system is guarded from the European level, the latter not being allowed to interfere with the national constitutional order. Thus, the national level is fenced off from the European level. Parliaments, which are no doubt fundamental to the constitutional structure of the member states, are then restricted to their own national level, also when they deliberate on EU matters and EU decision-making.

An alternative, polycentric way of interpreting this provision, is to understand it as a recognition of the importance and relevance of the values inherent in the constitutional structures of the member states to the EU constitutional order. Parliaments are a crucial element in the constitutional structure of the political and constitutional order of the member states of the European Union. By virtue of Article I-5 this element of the structure is declared part of the identity of the EU itself. Parliaments' role in legitimating democratically the exercise of power by public authorities in this view must of necessity also concern the exercise of power in the framework of, and on the basis of, EU decisions. National parliaments are not necessarily to be restrained only to whatever national authorities do or do not do within the remit of their responsibility, and to the extent of their accountability towards the national parliament in a strictly national one-to-one relationship. National parliaments also have a role to play in the structure of the EU itself.

This reading is reinforced by other provisions of the Constitutional Treaty. The provisions on subsidiarity, in particular, can be read in the light of the polycentric paradigm. The independent role envisaged for national parliaments is neatly brought out in the body of the Constitutional Treaty, by Article I-11 (3) which provides that the institutions of the EU are to apply the principle of subsidiarity, while the national parliaments are to ensure their compliance with it.[11] Subsidiarity is a principle which applies to the EU institutions and its agencies and other bodies, but it is the national parliaments which scrutinise, determine, and hence supervise, whether the EU institutions apply it correctly.

This is confirmed by Article 6 (1) of the Protocol on the application of the principles of subsidiarity and proportionality, which provides for the possibility of national parliaments or a chamber thereof 'to send to the Presidents of the European Parliament, the Council and the Commission a reasoned opinion stating why it considers that the draft in question does not comply with the principle of subsidiarity'. The significant element here, as elsewhere in the protocol, is that the parliaments (or chambers thereof) are placed in a direct and unmediated relation to the European institutions. They do not address their views on a draft EU measure to their own national government, nor are their views to

---

11 Article I-11 (3), indent 2, provides that 'the institutions of the Union shall apply the principle of subsidiarity as laid down in the Protocol on the application of the principles of subsidiarity and proportionality. National Parliaments shall ensure compliance with that principle in accordance with the procedure set out in that Protocol'.

be transmitted by their governments, but they immediately communicate with the EU institutions. National parliaments are thus made actors with their own independent role to play within the EU constitutional system. They are made an integral part of a truly composite constitutional order.

A new feature of the subsidiarity protocol is the possibility of bringing actions to the European Court of Justice. The relevant provision is Article 8.[12] The first part of this provision suggests little that is new, in as much as it provides for actions for infringements of the principle of subsidiarity being brought by member states in accordance with Article III-365 of the Constitutional Treaty.[13] The very same paragraph of Article 8 immediately adds, however, that the ECJ shall also have jurisdiction in cases '*notified* by [the member states] in accordance with their legal order on behalf of their national Parliament or a chamber of it'. The language is interesting, because it reveals that apart from the actions by *member states* under Article III-365, there is also to be a different action, although it is not called an 'action', which is that by a national parliament or a chamber of it. The reason for considering this a separate type of member state action, different from the one by 'member states', is that it does not emanate from the government, as is usually the case, but that it is an action which is merely to be 'notified by' the relevant member state, read: government. This means that as regards the national parliaments, the protocol here 'pierces the veil' of the member state. Member states are at the EU level represented by the governments in accordance with the general rules and principles of public international law. However, here the protocol makes clear that it is *not* the government or member state which is actually bringing the action, but the *parliament* or a chamber of it: the government merely 'notifies' it. Parliaments are thus recognised as true actors within the EU constitutional order, also *vis-à-vis* the European Court of Justice under Article III-365 concerning the legality of acts of the EU institutions. National parliaments thus become true actors in their own right in the European Union, prised away from the grip of their governments in the particular context of European Union decision-making.

---

12 'The Court of Justice of the European Union shall have jurisdiction in actions on grounds of infringement of the principle of subsidiarity by a European legislative act, brought in accordance with the rules laid down in Article III-365 of the Constitution by Member States, or notified by them in accordance with their legal order on behalf of their national Parliament or a chamber of it.' In accordance with the rules laid down in the said Article, the Committee of the Regions may also bring such actions against European legislative acts for the adoption of which the Constitutional Treaty provides that it be consulted.

13 Article III-365 (1) provides for review by the Court of Justice of the European Union of the legality of European laws and other acts producing legal effects. Article III-365 (2) of the Constitutional Treaty provides that 'for the purposes of paragraph 1, the Court of Justice of the European Union shall have jurisdiction in actions brought by a Member State, the European Parliament, the Council or the Commission on grounds of lack of competence, infringement of an essential procedural requirement, infringement of the Constitution or of any rule of law relating to its application, or misuse of powers'.

6 Opening up to Accountability

When we compare the 'multilevel' and the 'polycentric' paradigm, the latter seems, at least theoretically, to offer more opportunities for national parliaments to be involved in EU affairs, thus contributing to a broader democratic legitimacy of the EU institutions' work. To the EU institutions themselves it offers chances for opening up to accountability in contexts in which to date they have not done so save in exceptional cases. This state of affairs is inherent in the 'model' of relations between national institutions and EU institutions of each of these paradigms. Let us have a closer look at the possibilities and limits of each.

In the 'levels' approach, the EU institutions constitute an autonomous level, and the national institutions are restricted within their autonomous level. This means that what happens at one level can be understood properly in the terms of reference of that level only. To put it more concretely, members of the Council are understood only in terms of EU law, and are hence viewed exclusively as members of a European institution. Viewed from the level of the EU, it is merely coincidental that these members happen to be also in a position of ministerial responsibility towards their respective national parliaments, at least in the cases where the member state representative is a minister. If the representative in the Council is actually a member of a state or regional executive within a federal or decentralised member state, as is regularly the case with Germany, Belgium,[14] Austria and the UK, then political responsibility is not articulated at national level but at sub-national level; if the representative in the Council is a civil servant, like a Permanent Representative or another civil servant, the official actually participating in the Council meetings is himself not responsible to the parliament of the relevant member state but to his national minister, who in turn is in principle accountable to his national parliament. In the European Council, the heads of state who form part of it are not accountable to the parliament of the member state they head, but the heads of government are. The actual modalities and possibilities for holding representatives to account before national parliaments differ, and the possibilities and modalities of sanctioning their responsibility differ even more. But from the perspective of the EU level all this is an irrelevant coincidence when we view things within the 'levels' paradigm. Within this paradigm, political accountability is indeed an issue, but the only thing which matters in this regard is the rules of the EU constitution as embodied in the constitutional principles of the treaties and constitutional practice at EU level, *viz.* (1) that the Council can be heard in the European Parliament on the basis of conditions which the Council determines in its own rules of procedure;[15] (2) that there is no relation of accountability between the Euro-

[14] See the contribution by Wouter Pas in this volume.

pean Council and the European Parliament; and (3) that otherwise it is only the Commission which can be held to account, and be sanctioned for the political responsibility it holds.[16] All the rest is a matter for the national level.

Within the 'levels' paradigm, accountability for what representatives have done or failed to do in the Council is a matter based exclusively on national constitutional law. At national level, in turn, a minister is viewed merely as a minister who happened to have sat in the Council, not as a member of the Council; representatives who happen to be ministers of the states within a federation are primarily considered to be governed by the prevailing federal principles; and representatives who are civil servants are (generally) not politically responsible, but their political principal, usually a minister, is so by imputation on the basis of national constitutional law. Accountability exists only to the extent that it is engaged under national constitutional law for what happens to have been done or failed to be done in a more or less fortuitous exterior forum.

Under the 'polycentric' paradigm, by contrast, the EU and national institutions are viewed as forming part of one constitutional order. What happens in EU institutions can be immediately relevant to the national institutions, also in terms of accountability. The fact that Council members are principally ministers is no coincidence, and is of consequence for parliamentary accountability. The *dédoublement fonctionnel* with regard to representatives in the Council and European Council is not accidental but essential; it is essential to EU decision-making to be an object of accountability and hence to acquire legitimacy, not only within the closed terms of EU law in the strict sense, but throughout the whole of the constitutional order which comprises the member state constitutional orders as well. 'Points of contact' and interaction between EU and national political acts, and actors, exist in the polycentric approach to a much larger extent than they do in the levels approach. Accountability is then *not* a matter of separate levels, but a matter which extends throughout the political and constitutional order, and touches both the EU system in the narrow sense and the national systems.[17]

---

15 Article 197 (4) EC: 'The Council shall be heard by the European Parliament in accordance with the conditions laid down by the Council in its Rules of Procedure.'

16 Article 197 (2) and (3), and 201 EC; here constitutional practice comes into play as well. This became most evident at the failure of the initially proposed members of the Barroso Commission to acquire the consent of the European Parliament, notwithstanding the fact that the Treaty does not explicitly grant them the power to veto Commission members proposed by the governments of the member states. For a detailed description of the events, and a constitutional analysis, see 2 *European Constitutional Law Review* (2005) 153-280.

17 This is again evidenced by the Barroso affair as discussed in the various articles in *EuConst*, footnote 16 *supra*.

7 Opportunities without a Constitutional Treaty

We have pointed out some features of the Treaty establishing a Constitution for Europe which fit better with the polycentric than with the 'multilevel' approach. As this Treaty will in the short term not enter into force in the manner foreseen, the question arises whether what the polycentric paradigm promises can be realised, a question which also 'tests' whether we are in fact dealing with a paradigm or only an ideological contrivance which does not have any explanatory and heuristic power beyond the text of this one normative instrument of the Constitutional Treaty.

With regard to political accountability towards parliaments, national parliaments can certainly escape from the limitations which inhere in the 'multilevel' view. The possibilities which already exist for national parliaments are several:

- From various sides it has been pointed out that the 'yellow card' procedure under the Constitutional Treaty's subsidiarity protocol can also be put in place even if the Treaty does not enter into force. National parliaments could in practice act voluntarily in accordance with the provisions of the protocol also before, and even without its entry into force. In an inter-institutional agreement, the Commission could bind itself to the practice of reconsidering, or withdrawing, a proposal if it receives too many negative views from national parliaments regarding the proposal's appropriateness in the light of the principle of subsidiarity.
- There is as such no restriction for national parliaments to express views and address them to whichever of the EU institutions, bodies and agencies they find relevant. The French amended their constitution (entering into force as of the entry into force of the EU Constitutional Treaty), this time not to enable the national parliament to express itself towards its government, but to express itself towards the European Parliament, the Council and the Commission on whether EU proposals are in accordance with the principle of subsidiarity.[18] Other national parliaments might similarly remove national constitutional obstacles for expressing themselves on EU matters towards the EU institutions, should there be such obstacles – probably there are none. By doing so, parliaments could break out from the self-imposed restriction to the national context as the only relevant one even in relation to EU matters.
- National parliaments can on the basis of national law force their govern-

[18] *Loi* 2005-204 of 1 March 2005, Article 88-5 of the constitution is due to read, as from the entry into force of the EU Constitutional Treaty: 'L'Assemblée nationale ou le Sénat peuvent émettre un avis motivé sur la conformité d'un projet d'acte législatif européen au principe de subsidiarité. L'avis est adressé par le président de l'assemblée concernée aux présidents du Parlement européen, du Conseil et de la Commission de l'Union européenne. Le Gouvernement en est informé. [...] A ces fins, des résolutions peuvent être adoptées, le cas échéant en dehors des sessions, selon des modalités d'initiative et de discussion fixées par le règlement de chaque assemblée.'

ment to bring a case to the ECJ. In Germany there is a legislative basis for bringing a case at the ECJ at the request of the *Bundesrat* in the context of the federal division of powers; in France, an explicit constitutional basis for doing so at the request of either house of parliament, in the context of an alleged infringement of subsidiarity, has been created.[19] In other countries, the forces of the parliamentary system of government could, and should, lead governments to bring an action at the request of a parliamentary majority spontaneously. Should this create difficulties, national legislation can be passed to create an obligation for governments to do so. The duty for a government to bring an action at the ECJ need not be restricted to cases concerning an alleged infringement of the principle of subsidiarity, or to matters which touch states' prerogatives in federal member states. In unitary countries, as in federal states, it is the national parliament's prerogative to exert legislative power, and hence, under a

---

19 Cf. Germany, *Gesetz* (based on *Grundgesetz* Article 23 (7)) *über die Zusammenarbeit von Bund und Ländern in Angelegenheiten der Europäischen Union* of 1993, § 7: '(1) Die Bundesregierung macht auf Verlangen des Bundesrates unbeschadet eigener Klagerechte der Länder von den im Vertrag über die Europäische Union vorgesehenen Klagemöglichkeiten Gebrauch, soweit die Länder durch ein Handeln oder Unterlassen von Organen der Union in Bereichen ihrer Gesetzgebungsbefugnisse betroffen sind und der Bund kein Recht zur Gesetzgebung hat. Dabei ist die gesamtstaatliche Verantwortung des Bundes, einschließlich außen-, verteidigungs- und integrationspolitisch zu bewertender Entwicklungen zu wahren. (2) Absatz 1 gilt entsprechend, wenn die Bundesregierung in Verfahren vor dem Europäischen Gerichtshof Gelegenheit zur Stellungnahme hat. (3) Hinsichtlich der Prozeßführung vor dem Europäischen Gerichtshof stellt die Bundesregierung in den in den Absätzen 1 und 2 genannten Fällen sowie für Vertragsverletzungsverfahren, in denen die Bundesrepublik Deutschland Partei ist, mit dem Bundesrat Einvernehmen her, soweit Gesetzgebungsbefugnisse der Länder betroffen sind und der Bund kein Recht zur Gesetzgebung hat'; as well as the *Vereinbarung vom 29. Oktober 1993 zwischen der Bundesregierung* und den Regierungen der Länder über die Zusammenarbeit in Angelegenheiten der Europäischen Union in Ausführung von § 9 des Gesetzes vom 12. März 1993 über die Zusammenarbeit von Bund und Ländern in Angelegenheiten der Europäischen Union: 'V. Verfahren vor den Europäischen Gerichten. (1) Im Hinblick auf die hier zu wahrenden Verfahrensfristen unterrichtet die Bundesregierung den Bundesrat unverzüglich von allen Dokumenten und Informationen über Verfahren vor dem Europäischen Gerichtshof und dem Gericht erster Instanz, an denen die Bundesregierung beteiligt ist. Dies gilt auch für Urteile zu Verfahren, an denen sich die Bundesregierung beteiligt. (2) Macht die Bundesregierung bei Vorliegen der Voraussetzungen von § 7 Abs. 1 EUZBLG auf Beschluß des Bundesrates von den im Vertrag über die Europäische Union vorgesehenen Klagemöglichkeiten Gebrauch, so fertigt sie die entsprechende Klageschrift. Von den Ländern wird hierfür rechtzeitig eine ausführliche Stellungnahme zur Sache zur Verfügung gestellt. (3) Nr. 2 gilt entsprechend, wenn die Bundesregierung in Verfahren vor dem Europäischen Gerichtshof Gelegenheit zur Stellungnahme hat.' See also the French constitution, Article 88-5 (2), in its envisaged wording under the 2005 *Loi*, see footnote 18 *supra*: 'Chaque assemblée peut former un recours devant la Cour de justice de l'Union européenne contre un acte législatif européen pour violation du principe de subsidiarité. Ce recours est transmis à la Cour de justice de l'Union européenne par le Gouvernement.'

division-of-powers reasoning, most legislative measures of the EU may potentially come within the purview of this prerogative power, and thus affect national parliaments. All justiciable matters which can be entertained at the ECJ can therefore potentially be the subject matter of a duty to bring an action on behalf of a national parliament, such as substantive legality, legal basis, subsidiarity, but also the failure of the EU institutions to respect the time limits allowing for scrutiny as laid down in the Protocol on the national parliaments of 1997, which failure would affect the rights of national parliaments under the protocol.

- Members of the European Parliament can, and do, in various manners, and to various degrees, participate in the work of national parliaments, their committees, and the political groups therein. Much has been done about obstacles in this respect, whether they be perceived or real. Attention should also be paid to participation of members of national parliaments in the work of the European Parliament. This is not necessarily a matter of having a 'double mandate' of membership in both the European and the national parliament.
- In national parliaments, ministers are at present held to account only as regards what they have achieved, or failed to achieve, in the Council as national ministers. But this is a very restricted stance which enables ministers to withdraw themselves from accountability for the decisions which are actually taken by the Council. To remedy this, national parliaments should consider their ministers as representatives *of the Council* and hold them to account as such, and not solely and merely as representatives of the member state in some external forum: they are not, as any EC lawyer will admit.
- Similarly, national parliaments should also hold other EU institutions than the Council to account. It is too rare for the Commission president or individual commissioners to defend their views in a national parliament.[20] There is no reason why national parliaments or their committees should not in relevant cases also invite representatives of the other institutions to defend theirs in relevant cases.

If they are to play a role in the European constitutional order of which they are to be fully part, national parliaments must consider the EU institutions as immediate counterparts. Obviously, national parliaments do not provide the only institutional path along which accountability for the EU can be mobilised, nor is that

[20] A recent example is the appearance of Commission president Barroso in the French Assemblée Nationale on 24 January 2006, in which he gave a speech on the state of the European Union and answered questions from one member of each political group; see *Le Monde*, 'M. Barroso s'explique devant les députés français', 25 January 2006, p. 8. For an impression of the very lively debate see news clip at http://videos.tf1.fr/video/news/newsthemes/france/0,,3280574,00.html. For a full report see www.assemblee-nationale.fr/international/barroso.asp.

the only manner to provide the EU with legitimacy – far from it. But only if the national parliaments conceive of the EU institutions and themselves as partners and counterparts in the body politic of the Union can the EU descend from its high-level stance and open up to accountability outside its own restricted framework at the EU level.

8 A Research Agenda

The change in paradigm on which the above analysis builds gives rise to many further questions which for lack of space are not dealt with here. A number of issues for further research must, however, be specified for a proper, in-depth investigation of the possibilities of national parliaments within the larger context of the EU as a polycentric composite constitutional order.

The actual and potential roles of national parliaments need to be analysed in a more differentiated manner than has happened so far. This can be done along three different axes (which systematically relate such roles to the different types of EU competence) to the various forms of decision-making procedures, which are related to the different instruments in which decision-making results, and to the different European actors involved in the process. As regards the types of EU competence, both practice and the literature have suggested that the national parliaments have more of a role to play when it concerns non-exclusive EU powers and shared powers, than when it concerns exclusive powers. This hypothesis needs testing. It seems to focus strongly on 'input' legitimacy which national parliaments can provide in terms of their powers at the national level. As regards the forms of EU instruments and decision-making procedures, there is a plethora of modalities. Instruments range from treaties, EC instruments, Second and Third Pillar instruments, to benchmarking and reporting within the open method of co-ordination. Decision-making procedures range from 'normal' legislative procedures involving Commission, Council and European Parliament, via delegated executive procedures known as comitology, to informal co-operation. In this respect attention needs also to be drawn to the prevalent idea that (the possibility to resort to) majority voting influences the role which national parliaments can play. If this is true, it needs further investigation in what manner it does so, and what this implies.

As regards the decision-making actors, we have already made a number of suggestions and remarks in the previous sections of this essay. Here I draw attention to the relation with the role attributed to the European Parliament, but which is also relevant for the role of national parliaments with regard to exclusiveness of competence and the type of decision-making procedure. Two main approaches are taken both in the literature and in practice. The first approach views the relationship between national parliaments and the European Parliament as mutually exclusive, and regards the legitimising and accountability function of national parliaments to be sufficiently exhausted wherever the

European Parliament has a formal decisive role; little or no room is left for a meaningful role of national parliaments. The other approach considers the two parliaments as complementary, the European Parliament fulfilling a role at the EU level which is not, and cannot be, identical to the role of national parliaments with regard to EU issues.

The theoretical analysis and assessment of these views on the respective roles of national and European parliaments may hinge crucially on the difference in the two paradigms sketched. Nevertheless, independently of such a normative approach it would be useful to see whether in practice national parliaments which ostensibly hold one of these views (a case in point being the Netherlands, where parliament ostensibly only sees a scrutinising role for itself when the European Parliament has no or few powers) still make use of practices of scrutiny or other forms of discussing and reviewing EU decision-making. The more differentiated analysis outlined here should make it possible not only to clarify present roles, but also to suggest new opportunities for national parliaments in the polycentric setting of EU decision-making itself.

9 Concluding Remarks

Exchanging the compartmentalised multilevel approach for a more inclusive polycentric understanding of the composite constitutional order of the European Union changes the perspective on the relevance and role of national parliaments in the EU. We have emphasised the opportunities this offers for opening up the EU to accountability and enhancing its legitimacy. But greater opportunities are no guarantee that they will be used. In fact, one may expect that the putting into operation of the subsidiarity mechanism as envisaged by the subsidiarity protocol to the Treaty establishing a Constitution for Europe may lead to an investment of scarce resources into one form of early scrutiny which will detract from existing and alternative mechanisms of national parliamentary scrutiny which are at least as far-reaching and meaningful, (or even more so) as the subsidiarity test alone. The subsidiarity test might thus well prove to be a great threat to the much broader role which national parliaments can and should play. In fact, it may force parliaments further into the 'levels' approach: once a matter is considered an EU matter, that is the end of a role for national parliaments, and only in the opposite case (a matter not being suitable for EU decision-making) is there a role for national parliaments.

Scarce resources in terms of time, facilities, budget, staffing, and expertise, are very real obstacles to a meaningful role for national parliaments already at present. They may well remain so in the future. Although paradigm shifts concern ways of viewing reality, and seem to that extent a 'mental' operation, this mental nature of the paradigm shift (or not) is ultimately not decisive. Constitutions do not only live through the ideals, ideas and models which inspire them. Whether or not constitutions exist meaningfully depends on the extent to which they are realised, have real existence through constitutional practice. Abiding by a constitution is not an act of piety, it requires action in real life. It is up to the parliaments themselves to realise the shift in paradigm. This requires a great effort on their part to overcome such practical obstacles as those mentioned. That there are several examples of national parliaments who have been able to do so, is proof that it can be done and should be an inspiration to others.

References

- P.K. Feyerabend, *Against Method* (London 1975).
- Th.S. Kuhn, *The Structure of Scientific Revolutions* (Chicago 1962).
- I. Pernice, 'Multilevel Constitutionalism and the Treaty of Amsterdam: European Constitution-Making Revisited', 36 *CMLRev* (1999) 703-750
- I. Pernice, 'Multilevel Constitutionalism in the European Union', 5 *ELRev* (2002) 511-529.